Much Like Joseph

FROM PIT TO GLORY

A SERVICE-DISABLED VETERAN'S MIRACULOUS LIFE STORY

A TRUE STORY

Desire Nana

TRILOGY CHRISTIAN PUBLISHERS

TUSTIN, CA

Trilogy Christian Publishers
A Wholly Owned Subsidiary of Trinity Broadcasting Network
2442 Michelle Drive
Tustin, CA 92780

Much Like Joseph

To my mom, Lydie Nana; my wife, Rachel Vira Nana; my daughters Maelo Menjene, Amarissa Nana, Raya Nana, and Abira Nana.

Endorsements

Desire Nana served as my religious program specialist in the Navy during combat deployments to the Arabian Gulf. I knew him then as a man of strong character and sincere faith. This is the story of how that character and faith were formed. From impoverished beginnings in his home country of Cameroon to the United States Navy and beyond, God has intervened in Desire's life on numerous occasions to make him the man he is today. That same God longs to intervene in your life too. As you read this story, may God touch your life in some similar way!

—Chaplain Michael Gore
CAPT, CHC, USN (Ret)

This book contains the gut-wrenching story of Desire Nana, a man I have come to highly respect. Heartbreak and misfortune are words that many would use to define his life, but Nana saw more. He saw Joseph, the son of Jacob, who persevered through trials because he knew that God was doing something greater than the calamity happening around him. Somehow, Nana saw past his circumstances and recognized the hand of God. His story is compelling and inspiring to all of us!

— Dr. Brian C. Hughes
Senior Pastor

Foreword

Nana's story is an amazing testimony of how God's grace and power can overcome evil and transform our everyday lives.

—Dr. Tim Clinton
President, American Association of Christian Counselors

Contents

Preface

Most of us think of people in the Bible as if they were not ordinary people like us. But what if I told you that my story in this book is similar to that of the great patriarch, Joseph, in the Old Testament?

God worked through my childhood, education, failures, chaos, and abuse to bring me from Cameroon to the Promised Land. He used my mom, a stranger, a teacher, some elders, and brothers in Christ to realize His plans for my life.

God used my mom as an unwavering moral and financial support. He used strangers to give me a place to stay when I was kicked out of the house, and He used one of His children to bring me to Him. He used a teacher to help me comprehend math like I had never understood before, which would help me complete my high school diploma. This would help me satisfy a requirement in my application to come to the US. He used brothers in Christ to help me complete forms.

By no means am I comparing myself to the great patriarch Joseph, but there are some similarities in our stories. I intend to glorify the name of the Lord and show how our great God works behind the scenes to change, bless, and transform His children.

Introduction

J oseph, in the Old Testament, was one of Jacob's twelve sons. His father loved him very much, more than the others, and gave him a colored cloak as a symbol of his love. His brothers grew jealous of their father's favoritism.

One day, Joseph told his brothers that he had dreamed there were binding sheaves of grain out in the field. Suddenly, his sheaf rose and stood upright. His brothers concluded that he was going to reign over them, which was true. They hated him even more than they already had.

Because of Joseph's brothers' jealousy, he was sold to slavery and taken to Egypt, where he would eventually become the right hand of Potiphar, a Pharaoh's official.

Because of Joseph's faithfulness to the Lord, he would refuse to be seduced by Potiphar's wife, which would result in Joseph going to prison after Potiphar's wife's false accusation. Due to his ability to interpret Pharaoh's dream, he was released from prison and became the governor of Egypt. As Governor, he was able to manage the country's goods to save it from years of famine.

Because of Joseph's faithfulness, the Lord kept him safe and fulfilled many promises to give him a bright future.

***

My future in Cameroon was uncertain.

After years of praying, I got my first job in 2001 with a French road construction company named SATOM, located in Douala, the economic capital of Cameroon. The job was to last four years. I put all my hopes and dreams into the job because I planned to save money to move out of the country.

I got hired as an electrician supervisor—number two behind a French expat named Bertrand (expats or expatriates are individuals coming from a different country to work on a specific project in a country other than their country of citizenship)—to supervise all electric works and electricians under me. The road construction project was in Bertoua in the eastern part of the country. The project was to join Cameroon and the Central African Republic.

I left my hometown of Douala to go to Bertoua to manage the electric department with Mr. Bertrand. The construction base had to be built from the ground up, so electricians, plumbers, and other tradesmen were needed to construct and maintain the housing apartments for expats.

When I got to the base for the first time, I met with Bertrand and other electricians on the jobsite. We introduced ourselves. Bertrand and one of the electricians, named Judah, did not seem happy to see me. But Bertrand had no choice but to welcome me on board because I had been hired by his boss, Mr. Giraud, who was the supervisor of all technical trades on the base. I would later learn that my presence was going to change an order already established in the electrical department, and I was going to mess things up. Mr. Giraud would later join me in Bertoua after he completed all hiring in Douala.

Just like Joseph—the famed favorite son of Jacob in the Old Testament book of Genesis—my story reveals betrayal and God's love. In addition to my presence changing the already established order, I would later learn that Bertrand and Judah did not like me because I was the youngest, the most educated, and the well-paid electrician on the team of five.

Judah undermined my leadership as soon as we started the work by damaging electrical equipment to make me look bad. He would spread false rumors about my competence when things went wrong.

Talking about leadership change, Judah believed I took his place as the number two on the team and did not want to take any orders from me. He had the support of Bertrand, who had hired him at the project location in Bertoua.

By God's grace, I was able to do my job very well and met every single installation challenge that we had on the base. Just as Joseph was known to interpret dreams, I was known in the base as a knowledgeable electrician, which did not please Judah and Bertrand. Judah would sabotage electrical systems, and I was able to fix any malicious electrical problems. Bertrand knew what was going on, but he did not say or do anything about it.

One thing they did not notice or know was that when they created electrical problems to challenge my knowledge or to sabotage me, I became more popular because I fixed it. The working conditions were stressful, but I leaned on the Lord. After two years and many failed sabotage attempts, their jealousy grew to hatred, and they started to formulate their plan to get me fired.

As a French foreigner, Bertrand had a good relationship with the base's director, who was a French foreigner as well. Bertrand was in charge of our evaluations and never gave me a good one. Those evaluations were influenced by Judah since they were friends. Judah and Bertrand had many things in common: both were womanizers, and they did not love the Lord. When Mr. Giroud was reassigned to another project out of the country and could no longer protect me, they jumped at the chance to get me fired.

I was the only one called to fix things around the base, so Judah and Bertrand thought they might lose their jobs because they became useless. Judah convinced Bertrand that I was too expensive and that I made them look bad. Bertrand was then successful in convincing the director that I was expensive. He claimed that everything was under control, so he could let me go to save money because my service was no longer needed. The director did not know what was going on in the field or who was doing what. He bought into Bertrand's assertion and fired me.

I packed all my belongings and went back to Douala.

Just as I did not like being fired, I do not believe that Joseph liked being thrown into a pit or being sold into slavery. The Bible is silent about Joseph's life ambitions, but as for me, I had put all my hopes into that job. My dream to leave the country in search of a better life had been crushed. That was my belief.

The time to question God's faithfulness kicked in, and I started to worry about my future. I had gotten my first job at thirty years old and believed there wouldn't be another opportunity. I believed that the only legal way I could leave Cameroon was as a student. The older I got, the slimmer the chance to be accepted into any school in Europe became. I limited myself to other possibilities and the power of God.

Even though my worries grew, and I could not find any answers to my questions, I resolved to trust the Lord.

Our blessings always parallel our life, and it is up to us to not disturb that by staying faithful to God. In the pages of this book, you will read in more detail my challenging story of abuse, chaos, God's revenge, and betrayal. You will also see my life's itinerary traced by God. Unlike Joseph, I disobeyed and paid the price. I learned from those mistakes.

I desire to glorify God and point you to the one who sees us and gives us the power to overcome, even when our life is much like Joseph's.

CHAPTER 1

Childhood

I was born in Cameroon in a city called Douala. Douala is the largest city in Cameroon. Douala has the largest port in Central Africa, and it also has a major international airport, Douala International Airport (DLA). Douala is the economic capital of Cameroon, and through its Airport and Port, it serves the entire CEMAC region comprising Gabon, Congo, Chad, Equatorial Guinea, Central African Republic, and Cameroon with goods. As of 2021, the city and its surrounding area had an estimated population of 3,793,363. Douala typically features warm and humid conditions with average annual temperatures ranging from 23° to 28° (73.4 to 82.4).

I have two brothers and two sisters. My late dad was a tailor, and my mom was a reseller. Neither spoke French, the primary language of the country. They only spoke our dialect, Medumba, which was the language spoke in our home. This made my early education very difficult.

I did not have any home educational support. Since my parents could not understand French, I was abandoned to myself, and I could not do my homework as I should. French was a foreign and second language to me, and this hindered any progress I could have made in school. I was still not able to read and write well by grade eight.

I struggled to express myself because I did not have full command of the French language. This put me in a disadvantaged position to communicate effectively and perform well in school to the best of my ability. In the process, my confidence was undermined. This led to emotional stress, which also affected my ability to learn.

The struggle was true throughout elementary and middle school, and this would later affect the cognitive, psychological, social-cultural aspects of my life. But I give a lot of credit to my mom. Even though we were a poor family and she could not help me with any schoolwork, she managed to send me to school, although I repeated a lot of grades.

She did her best to provide my siblings and me with one meal a day when she could. I knew the routine in every single house in the neighborhood, and some days

I would show up at a neighbor's house at mealtime to make sure I had something to eat.

We were very limited in what we could eat, and it depended on how successful my mom was at making money. A day with no profit meant a day with no food. Foods like beef and chicken were out of our reach, but my parents were able to save some money during the year so they could afford those prestigious foods during the holiday season, like Christmas and New Year.

My four siblings and I were very happy children, even though we never had birthday parties—or received any gifts, for that matter—because we did not know any better. Our contentment was the key to our happiness. We were not exposed to the outside world, and we did not have a TV at home to be able to compare our lifestyle with others.

However, we had a couple of neighbors who had a TV in their homes. Their houses were always packed, especially when there was a popular series on, like Knight Rider.

All our shoes, pants, and shirts were bought in the thrift stores, and the name brands were out of our reach. We rarely visited the pharmacy because their medications were too expensive. When necessary, our mom shopped at illegal corner pharmacies run by people who did not have the knowledge, experience, license, or degrees. They had all types of medications, and nobody knew the source. Sometimes those medications were out of date, but most people didn't know better, and we did not even know the danger. We had no choice, and we were fine with it. The illegal corner pharmacies are still open in Cameroon, and the owners of those stores are called "doctors."

There's no government aid for low-income families, no food stamps (SNAP Food Benefits), no welfare or temporary assistance for needy families (TANF), no Medicaid and children's health insurance program (CHIP), and no low-income housing. The government did not provide any help to its own people, so everyone had to work to feed his family or himself.

Most of our neighborhood was living in the same condition as us. The houses looked the same, we had the same issues, we looked the same, and we just believed and accepted our fate. To find a rich neighborhood, you had to go to the heart of a city, such as Bonajo and Akwa.

Our house was built with temporary material (wood), and it was seriously damaged with a lot of holes. Someone could have put his hand through the wood to pull us right out of the house if they had wanted to.

We did not have running water and had to walk miles to a fountain to get clean drinking water. Sometimes, we collected rain as drinking water. We had a traditional outside bathroom, and we used the well water to shower and cook. The well was deep, and we had to use a bucket attached to a rope to pull the water out, just like you see on TV.

Things did not change much as I was growing up. We still had only one meal a day.

In Cameroon, public and secondary public schools were supposed to be free, but they were not because corruption had affected every area of life. Education was no exception, and there were no free meals in school for the poor. Cameroon was ranked 153 out of 179 countries most corrupt in the world in 2020 by Transparency International.

There was supposed to be an entrance exam, especially in secondary school, but it was not always the case. School administrators had created a backchannel which they used to sell seats to the privileged families. As a poor kid, I could not get into a public school no matter how well I did in the entrance exam. This practice is still going on today, and in most cases, it has forced poor kids like me to attend private school or stay home if they could not afford tuition. This practice was a big burden on the poor families because they did not have any means to live, and now they had to pay for school.

This was one of many injustices inflicted on the poor citizens by the Cameroonian system.

My family was poor, and my mom had no choice but to pay for my secondary school education. My dad could have helped but chose not to.

My dad was absent from our childhood because he was addicted to alcohol. I cannot recall a time when he participated in paying my tuition.

Because my dad was not very involved, I had to do something to help my mom. I worked hard every summer break to make money to contribute to my tuition. Cameroon has a child labor law restricting minor children from working, but the law was not enforced by the government.

I started working at the age of ten as a sand carrier. I dug sand with my shovel and loaded it into trucks to make money. I also carried people's merchandise from the local market to their homes using a rented wheelbarrow.

It was the usual practice to get the wheelbarrow first and pay the rental fee at the end of the workday. One day, I rented a wheelbarrow, but I could not make any money. I came up with a plan to return the wheelbarrow without being noticed. I was lucky because the rental process did not involve any paperwork. It was just a verbal agreement.

I approached the rental place, made sure nobody was around, and dropped the wheelbarrow right in front of the rental store. I ran away without being noticed. Consequently, I could not go back to the same rental place to rent a wheelbarrow again. The next time I needed one, I went to a new place. The only thing I deplored about the situation was that I was not conscientious enough to do the right thing, which was to go back and pay the rental fee once I got some money.

My mom was a reseller of macabo (yams). She had to get up every morning at 4 a.m. and would wake me to be her bodyguard. I escorted her from our house to the taxicab station, where she could take a taxi to go buy her yams at the wholesaler. After she bought the yams, she would take another cab back to our local market-place, where she would resell them. Her dedication to her reselling business was absolute and resolute be-cause it was the only way she could pay for my educa-tion, put bread on the table, pay medical bills, and pur-chase needed items. She is my hero.

Mom was very smart in managing her money. I still cannot figure out how she was able to support us. Her yam business was not that lucrative, but at the begin-ning of every school year, she would come up with a lot of cash to pay for our tuition and school supplies.

The Lord put the love of school in my heart by push-ing me, even in my failure. Behind the scenes, He used my mom's dedication to accomplish one of the neces-sary requirements which would help me achieve my dreams.

My mom and dad came from farming families. Even though I was born in an urban area, Douala, my parents impacted the farming culture. For many school breaks, they sent me back to the village where they had both grown up and where my grandparents still lived. I was the oldest in my family, but I found myself being the youngest among my uncles in the village, with whom I would spend a few months of my break. They would make me do all types of farm work, including tending sheep.

Even though the Bible is not specific about Joseph's daily occupation before he got sold, I could imagine his acting as a typical teenager, being used by his brothers to do all sorts of things or tending the sheep when it was his turn like myself.

CHAPTER 2

Psychological and Emotional Abuse

My mom wanted the best for my siblings and me, and she knew our success was grounded in education and hard work. She did all she could to make me the man I am today. I learned that life was not easy, and it required hard labor and persistence.

My dad spent most of his money getting drunk, then abusing us. Most dads try to be good role models, but this was not the case for my dad.

I hated my dad's way of living and swore to be his complete opposite. He would call me names, humiliate me in front of everybody, reject me, degrade me, threaten me, put me down, belittle me, force me to walk miles to get drinking water, and beat my mom in front of my siblings and me. I did not feel loved by my dad, and I did not receive any sympathy, affection, or empathy from him. In addition, my dad would hit, kick, whip, and punch us whenever we did something he did not like.

I was more affected by the abuse than my siblings due to my more daring and aggressive acts and attitude. When sent on an errand, I was not likely to do what was required of me.

I did not want to be like my dad, and I feared I might inherit some of those toxic behaviors. My problem with my dad was not the drinking part but the effect of the alcohol on him and on his family. My dad would come home at around 2 a.m., when we were in a deep sleep, and wake the entire household. My mom was scheduled to leave at 4 a.m. to go buy her merchandise.

Dad would tell us stories that did not even make sense, and he would beat anyone who tried to close their eyes while he was talking. He would go as far as beating us if we refused to wake up.

The abuse from my dad created a rebellious habit in me. His rule was that we were not to fall asleep while he was speaking, and we were spanked if we tried to sleep. This was one of the greatest family tortures I ever comprehended.

In addition, he had this bad habit of threatening us when we did something wrong before he left the house in the morning. He said things like, "Wait until I come back."

Those words made me live in fear and anxiety because I did not know what to expect from him when he came home. We had an eye focused on his arrival, and we left the house as soon as we saw him coming because we were expecting a beating.

Also, at night, my dad would kick us—including my mom—out of the house, and we would walk six miles to our aunt's house. It was not wise to walk outside at a certain time at night because we could have been attacked by an armed robber. Many people have lost their lives by trying to defy the odds. It was not a law in Cameroon not to walk outside at a certain hour of the night, but because of the security concerns in the neighborhood, people established that rule for protection. Our dad did not care about the risk of us being killed.

Sometimes, we spent more than a week at our aunt's house before getting our dad's permission to go back home.

My mom was gentle, loving, and self-controlled. She never raised her voice, and she never stood up to my dad. She was introverted. My mom was resilient, emotional, fragile, and vulnerable, but still, she remained strong through the different abuse she went through, and she never gave up on her call to motherhood because of us. A piece of advice I would never give to a woman in an abusive relationship to follow. Her daily routine was to get up in the morning and go buy her merchandise to resell. When she returned home, she cooked and made sure we all ate; then, she would then lie down on a mat to rest. My mom would cook more than one side dish for any soup to make sure everyone had something to eat. She still has the same routine today.

She left the house once or twice a week to go to a neighborhood or family meeting. She is a beautiful person, and most people would testify to her kindness.

When my father abused her, I felt powerless. I could not bear seeing her cry, and most of the time, we cried together. I shared and sympathized with her pain.

Most of our neighbors knew our house was a center for drama. If the issue was not between my mom and dad, it would be between my dad and me or my siblings. My father often followed me through the neighborhood and stopped me to punish me for some reason or other.

All the abuse created tension between my dad and me because I was the oldest child. This abuse went on until I was fourteen.

Later, his abuse enraged me and inspired retaliation.

I recall two incidents where our differences almost got physical. First, my mom was eight months pregnant, and dad wanted her to fill a hole between our apartment and the retaining wall. The project consisted of digging out dirt from an area that was around a mile from our house and carrying it with wheelbarrows back to our apartment.

My siblings and I did our best and filled the hole after a long day of work. We knew our dad would be happy at our accomplishment. Dad saw what we had done and asked us if our mom had participated. We said no. We explained that she could not participate because of her pregnancy.

He intended to abuse my mom, and I could not let it happen. I was fifteen and considered myself a man. So I gave my dad a warning not to touch my mom ever again, or he would hear from me directly.

Even though our relationship worsened, he stopped physically abusing my mom that day because he saw that I was ready to defend her. But the emotional, verbal, and psychological abuse—such as insulting, threatening, humiliating, and intimidating us and our mom—continued.

The second incident happened when my dad came home late one night, drunk. I was taking a shower in an open area in the back yard of the house with no fence separating our neighbors and us. The neighbors were asleep, so I thought I had no risk of being seen by anyone.

In the middle of the shower, here came my drunken dad, and he started asking me questions such as, "What are you still doing up when all your brothers are sleeping?"

He acted like he was very concerned about me when he saw me up late. He progressed toward me to attack me while he asked questions. My first instinct was to defend myself, and I did not want to make noise to attract the neighbors' attention. In self-defense, I threw the bar of soap, and it hit him in his right eye.

My fear became a reality when my dad woke the neighborhood by yelling, "Nana killed me!"

I ran into the house to dress and packed some of my belongings to go spend the rest of the night at my friend's parents' house, not far from our house. It was not the first time I ran or spent the night at their house.

The next morning, my dad went to the hospital and had a big bandage put on his right eye just to prove I really did bust it. Yes, my dad was a drama king, and he told everyone in the neighborhood I was the ultimate reason why he had only one eye now, even though it was not true.

He kept his bandage on for at least two weeks. When he finally removed it, his eye was fine. But his wish to humiliate me had been granted. I was known in the neighborhood as the boy who had busted his dad's eye. Some parents even advised their children not to befriend me anymore and to stay far away from me.

After a couple of weeks at my friend's house, I was able to go back home.

One thing my dad learned from the two experiences was that I was a grown man, and I was ready to stand and defend myself and my mom. I even started threatening him with the police because I knew that my dad did not know better, and it was just a scare tactic. The police never showed up when you called, even if you called for child abuse because it was the practice in Cameroon. They cited many reasons why they could not come. Their favorite answer when you called was that their gas tank was empty.

Everything continued to worsen between my dad and me, and we could not stand each other. There were two camps in the house: Mom, me, and my siblings, and my dad by himself in the other camp. I was the firstborn. There was a big gap between my little sister and me because my mom had lost two girls after me. I was really the only person capable of standing up for my mom to defend her.

Our family situation kept worsening to the point where we needed some intervention. In our culture, the extended family came together when there was a problem between a child and a dad to solve any issue between the two. But in my case, many meetings took place, and all were unsuccessful. We went years looking at each other as the enemy. I lost all hope of having a normal relationship with my dad.

I became like a flea on my father's feet, and I believed at the time that he wanted to get rid of me at all costs, but he couldn't. The only way to get rid of me was to kill me, but I didn't think he would go that far.

Because of my dad's conduct and behavior, my mom, my siblings, and I were exposed to all kinds of danger. As a boy, I could not understand my dad's behavior. Later, I learned that alcohol addiction is a bad sickness. Our family felt the emotional side effects, and our lives, behaviors, and attitudes changed forever because of my dad's alcohol problem.

I personally had disruptive behavior, tension, and a strained relationship with my dad, but I never considered myself a victim. The effects of his alcoholism made me unhealthy in many ways.

Just like Joseph, I was despised and the target of the effects of sin. My father's alcoholism caused him to commit heinous acts of torture. Joseph was sold into slavery because of his brothers' jealousy.

But someone more powerful than my dad or Joseph's brothers was working behind the scenes to help.

CHAPTER 3

Psychological and Emotional Impact

As a child and teenager, I did not notice any behavioral problems in myself. But as an adult, I exhibited depression, negative self-esteem, loneliness, and social isolation. I experienced four types of abuse in my life: neglectful, physical, verbal, and emotional. Those caused me to be a delinquent with a negative outlook on life, a negative perception of my future, a negative perception of life, and a lack of enjoyment.

The trauma produced internal and external symptoms. I was emotionally unstable, and I was consumed by fear. I could not trust anyone. The tendency to isolate manifested into low self-esteem, depression, and difficulty in establishing meaningful relationships. I was also addicted to alcohol and cigarettes, like my father. I took any substance to feel better.

There were days when I wanted to take my own life. I tried by hitting my head on a concrete block and overdosing on medication. But I did not have the courage to go through with it. Part of me still wanted to live.

I feared I'd be like my dad because I started exhibiting some of his abusive behaviors toward my friends, siblings, and especially girlfriends.

One time, a girlfriend went to visit a relative of hers, and we set the time for her to return. She chose to stay a little longer since the relative needed her help. I got frustrated like she was my property. We had no cell phones at the time, and there was no way I could know that she had extended the visit. I took my pain patiently, and I waited on the street I knew she would take to come back home. When I saw her coming, I went toward her, grabbed her by her hair, and hit her with my fist before she had the chance to explain herself.

When I noticed the damage I had done, I came to my senses and apologized. I realized I was like my dad, and it broke my heart. She was gracious enough to forgive me and gave me a second chance, but our relationship was stained. The image of that scene is still fresh in my mind like it was yesterday.

My family was not spared. I yelled at my brothers and sisters, and I got into a fight with my youngest brother. I also brought my anger to the street.

One night, I went to a party and got drunk. I passed out near an outside toilet and spent all night there. Outside toilets in Cameroon and in some other countries in Africa were nasty at the time because they were not properly maintained. When I got up in the morning, I was the subject of mockery in the neighborhood, and I almost got into a fight with some of my neighbors. Even though I didn't hit anyone, I was always looking for an opportunity to get even.

I recall another incident where I went to the fountain to get some drinking water, and I met two young girls. The girls were in the front of the line. I got in front of them, and they tried unsuccessfully to stop me. They ran to get their two big brothers, who attacked me and kicked me in the face so many times that I was seriously hurt with blood running down my nose. Because I was outnumbered, I ran home for a safe haven, where I got punished for getting into a fight and not returning with any drinking water.

I was not a forgiving boy, and I always got my revanche, so I planned for the girls and especially their brothers to pay because they had broken my nose and had gotten me in trouble with my dad. I came up with a strategy to ambush the girls and their big brothers while they were coming back from school. I knew their school itinerary. I had some delinquent friends join me in this endeavor.

Our plan was to hide, wait, and attack them on their way home from school. I knew what time they would be dismissed from school, and I knew approximately at what time they would reach our hiding spot so we could attack.

Everything worked as planned, and as soon as we saw them coming, we got out of the bush to confront the girls and their brothers. They were very surprised by a group of people coming out of the bush to attack them, and I could see the fear in their eyes. It didn't take them long to realize who I was and the reason behind our attack.

Since my real objective was to avenge the brothers, my friends and I went on the attack by throwing punches and elbowing and kicking them. The brothers defended themselves by throwing punches at us too.

One of my friends had a reputation as a good fighter, and I remember seeing him hit one of the brothers more than four times under the jaw and on the nose, and he was seriously hurt and bleeding. The sisters ran to get some support in their neighborhood. As soon as their reinforcements showed up, everything changed because all my friends in the neighborhood came out as well.

People used baseball bats, knives, leather belts, and anything they could swing or throw. The fight between the two neighborhoods got crazy. A lot of people got hurt, and there was blood everywhere.

Things happened so quickly that I started to feel guilty about the chaos I had created. As soon as the police got involved, I disappeared from the scene and hid for at least a week. After a little investigation, someone told the police that I was the mastermind behind all the chaos. They looked for me because I had orchestrated the fight, but not even my parents knew where to find me.

One of the main differences between Joseph's story and mine is that he was raised by a good God-fearing parent. The Bible is silent about his teenage years, but he spent them with dysfunctional brothers who wanted him dead. I was raised in a dysfunctional family with parents who did not know the Lord and, worse, with an abusive father.

Unlike Joseph, whose family background predicted a bright future, my background predicted a failure, according to many people.

The similarities—Joseph's life changed drastically, and so did mine.

CHAPTER 4

Non-believer

Life was fun and miserable at the same time. Everything was permissible with no boundaries. I could say or do what I wanted, even if it hurt someone's feelings. I was proud, perverted, arrogant, a drinker, and a smoker. Everything was my way or no way.

I had a defensive attitude, especially when someone told me that I behaved just like Dad. My skin and eyes would turn red, and I was always ready to jump at the person and start a fight because I did not like to be compared to my dad.

My role models had a negative influence on my life. I felt fatherless because my dad was seldom there. Or worse, he was there, but he abused me, which resulted in my being unstable because I moved from house to house to stay safe. I was so disrespectful to my dad, and

I did not honor him as God would want. I was known by the entire neighborhood to be a rebellious child.

One day, my dad kicked me out after a fight. I thanked God for Mr. Innocent, one of our neighbors. He provided a place for me to live.

Since I did not have any boundaries or any moral standing, I committed all types of harmful behaviors, including stealing, fornication, lying, worshipping skulls, and many more.

I spent most of my summer break wondering what I was going to do since there were not many opportunities for jobs. I became dependent on my mom, and I spent some of my days at the local bar talking with friends and playing games of chance and expecting someone to buy me a beer. I was not productive, and I couldn't help myself and my family. The situation created family tension because I was useless and unproductive.

As a consequence, I was poor and psychologically anxious. I had poor health, I was stressed, and I was socially irresponsible, which eroded my self-confidence. I was also prone to taking risks—such as committing larceny—and I tended to discount my future because there was no hope.

I started to steal money from my mom. My room was next to hers, and the wall separating the two rooms was incomplete. There was enough space between the ceiling and the wall for me to crawl through and find me some money. No matter how well she would hide it, I would manage to find it. She always complained about her missing money. Every time she complained, I acted like I did not know what was going on.

I did not, however, bring this set of skills to the street. In Cameroon, there was something called "popular justice." When someone got caught stealing, the thief was burned alive under the nose of powerless law enforcement officers.

In God's eyes, I was a fornicator. I had sexual relationships with multiple girls out of marriage, which created a type of soul tie that took me years to be able to cut.

I was also an idol (ancestor skull) worshipper.

Cameroon has over two hundred and forty tribes, and I belong to the Bamileke tribe in the west part of the country. The Bamileke area grass field people are the largest ethnic group occupying the country's west and northwest regions. We are arranged under numerous groups, each under the authority of a chief or fon.

Most Bamileke believe in the power of ancestors, through the worshipping of their skull, to cause good affluence upon their descendants. Ten years after a parent died, the skull was exhumed and placed in a carefully built location. It was used to communicate with the spirits of the dead, as well as their godhead, to receive spiritual guidance. It was called the skull cult.

The action of worship was realized through a ritual of slaughtering animals, then pouring their blood on the ground where the skeleton was located, like the slaughter of animals in the Old Testament. After slaughtering an animal, skull worshippers process their bodies according to their ancestors' recommendation. Ancestors are believed to be especially prone to anger when this act of worship is not completed.

Ancestors' anger was translated into several forms of curses, like not being successful in life, sickness, bad luck, no job, not being able to bear a child, and more. After a sacrifice was made, people still felt like nothing was working in their life because there was no tangible change. Some people's beliefs persist today.

Many Bamileke decided to follow Christ because, in Him, they found the truth.

People did not find out their ancestor was mad against them by themselves. There was a middleman called a "marabout," who consulted spirits on their behalf. There was a process, which was through a marabout, to determine why nothing was working in one's life.

Generally, when people noticed life was not going according to their wishes and plans, they consulted a marabout. The marabout, in turn, invoked a supernatural power or spirit to find the source of their concerns. After he consulted the supernatural power, he was able to tell them the origin of their problems, according to the marabout seeker.

Personally, I never consulted a marabout, even though I would face some difficulties when I finished with school, such as finding employment. (My employment problems would continue until I became a Christian.) But my parents did on many occasions. They would contact a marabout on my behalf as well, without my consent.

I noticed that revelations provided by marabouts were not always true. As a matter of fact, most of those revelations were fabricated lies or hoaxes.

Marabouts' revelations divided families, turned people against each other, and damaged people's reputations. I recall two major incidents.

The first happened when I was a teenager, and my little sister was hit and killed by a car while going to school. According to my grandmother, the incident was so violent that my little sister's brain wound up on the road.

Before the incident, we went on vacation to our native village of Bazou to spend time with our grandparents. My little sister became attached to my grandmother. So when the vacation was over, we headed back to Douala and left my little sister behind.

One day, my mother got the news that my little sister had been hit by a car while walking to school. She was told that the driver of the car was my aunt's husband. The whole family was shocked and overwhelmed by the odd situation, and my mother was inconsolable.

We wondered why a situation like this could happen to us. We could not find any answers, so my mom visited the marabout to find out what had happened to her baby.

In Cameroon, there was no such thing as an accident because an accident was always believed to have been caused by a supernatural power. The marabout did what he did best, which was to trick my mom by using her own words to give her an answer.

According to my mom, during her consultation with the marabout, he asked her if she had a family member who drove a white car, knowing there was a good chance that someone in our family did.

My mom answered, "Yes. My brother."

My mom's oldest brother was named Mr. Nana, and I was named after him. He had raised my mother, given her in marriage, and assisted her during my little sister's funeral. My mom had already made it public to members of our family that he was the one to blame for my sister's death, so most fingers were pointing at him during the ceremony.

My baby sister's real killer—my mother's little sister's husband—was off the hook because the finger was being pointed at my uncle because of the marabout.

A few years after losing my little sister, I noticed that something was not right with my mother's relationship with her big brother.

We had at one time spent at least two weekends a month at my uncle's home. After my sister's death, the visits stopped, and communication also stopped. My mom asked us not to talk about him anymore. She did not mention the reason. So I went years without visiting my uncle. I could not do anything about the situation as a boy, and I had no choice but to go along with the family decision.

When I became aware of the full situation, I asked my mom how she could explain the fact that an accident had happened two hundred kilometers away from where my uncle lived, involving a different person with a different car model and color. She had no answer, but she believed the marabout and managed to accuse her big brother. The question troubled me for years, but I did not have the courage to confront my parents with any more tough questions.

It would not be until the Lord opened my eyes that I was able to see the enemy's hand behind this situation.

The second incident was less serious. After a day of reselling her merchandise, my mom came home very tired and misplaced her wallet with her entire revenue inside. She placed it on top of the mosquito net over her bed instead of keeping it in the usual place.

Her nightly routine to get ready for the next morning was to make sure the money to buy the merchandise was within reach. That night, she could not locate her wallet, and it created a sense of panic in her. She went wild and screamed, "Who took my money?"

My sister and I joined the search to find her wallet, but after hours of searching, we could not locate it. Since the search turned out to be in vain, and the issue could not be resolved by human power, my mom once again solicited the help of a marabout. Because it was too late at night, she visited her supernatural man the next morning to find out what had happened to her money.

After visiting the marabout, she came back home and pointed her finger at me. According to my mom, the marabout said that as soon as she came home the previous night, she put her money on top of the dresser, accessible to anyone, and her first son took it and spent as much as he could, but that he still had the rest of the unspent money on him. My mom believed him, and she asked me to at least return the rest of the money.

I was stunned by my mom's accusation. I had stolen money from her before, but not her capital. This accusation was not based on any fact. I knew I had not taken her money, and I also knew my siblings had not done it.

The question remained, what happened to the money? My siblings and I decided to give it a second look.

We searched suitcases, turned down the bed, opened every drawer, and checked any unconventional area in the room—nothing. We almost gave up; then, we asked ourselves where the only place we had not checked in this room was. And it was the top of the mosquito net. Who would imagine looking up there? Nobody, but we looked up there out of curiosity, and there was the entire wallet with every single penny in it.

My mom had given up searching because she believed the marabout, even though they had been proven wrong in the past. To her surprise, we gave her the wallet with all the money inside. She cried a joyful cry, and she asked for my forgiveness.

I thought this experience would create resentment toward marabouts, but it did not. At least my mom was aware that they could be wrong, and that was a good step in the right direction.

This practice of consulting a marabout in every life circumstance has dominated the Cameroonian culture. They believe that a marabout can resolve any life problem or point you to something that could help you. For example, marabouts were used to find a job, to get pregnant, to get a promotion at work, to become a member of the government, and more. They even used the practice to eliminate competition or rivals, to make someone's life miserable, and to eliminate a political opponent.

Those phenomena have affected the entire country. Most people did not count on themselves to bring about change in their life but subscribed to the idea that marabouts were their savior.

Poverty, caused by a supernatural reason beyond their control, was the main reason people believed they could not make it. Therefore, they became vulnerable to anyone who preached deliverance.

One thing people ignored was that marabouts created tricks to successfully make people believe they were in a position to help.

I was not a Christian, but it was obvious that people had a need to know God. They were, and still are, looking for deliverance in the wrong place and at the con artist.

Another example of a con artist was the brother-in-law of my first daughter's mother, Jenette.

When I moved to Bangangte, I had a neighbor who was also named Nana. We had the same last name, hailed from the same village, spoke the same dialect, and lived two feet away from each other.

My connection with Mr. Nana was instantaneous, and I had access to his house. He was open as to what he did for a living—he was a marabout. On multiple occasions, he told me all his tricks and how he fooled people into believing in his practice. He lied and scammed people for a living. Some marabouts could connect with evil spirit power, but they could not resolve a human's spiritual or physical needs.

He told me he did not have any supernatural power but that he was successful in making people believe by creating an illusion. For example, he made people believe he had a spiritual master in a different African country, Ghana, where he went to get resources. Then he traveled to Ghana to buy a bottle of perfume. He would present the bottle of perfume to his follower as a magic potion to resolve or help discover the mysteries responsible for his follower's misery.

He said he answered many of his followers' concerns by taking words out of their mouths. He would ask a lot of questions to know the background then formulate some answers to tell what was going on in their life. His followers would think he was a miracle worker.

He sent me to kill little reptiles for his practice, and I found it odd, but I did it anyway. He had such a great reputation, and he was known by kings and elites of the region.

After a while, unbeknownst to Mr. Nana and his wife, I started dating Mr. Nana's sister-in-law, who lived with them. My relationship with Mr. Nana was good until he found out I was going out with his wife's little sister, Jenette, and that she had become pregnant.

I was glad for the short relationship I had with Mr. Nana because it helped me know to see the truth through the eye of a belief system that had dominated the Cameroonian culture. This solidified my belief about marabouts—they were nothing but crooks extorting from the ignorant and poor.

I believed that when life was not going my way, when things were tough, or when everything was not going as planned, that I should ask why. I did not believe a marabout was or is the best person to go to for the answer to my question.

By exposing me to marabouts' practices, the Lord was setting and preparing me to be His witness among my friends and other people, who believed that marabouts were the only ones to whom they could go for help.

Marabouts were considered to be miracle workers who made one's life better. But from my personal experience, I made up my mind as an adolescent not to go down that road no matter what life threw at me because marabouts did more harm than good.

I didn't know there was a Savior waiting for me to cast all my problems on Him. Marabouts seemed like the only option for many.

Even though I was not a Christian, I still remember the first encounter I had with the Lord Jesus, but at the time, I did not know who the guy being beaten in the movie was.

This was how everything went down for me as a young man. I was always partying with friends, especially during the Christmas season.

One Christmas, my friends and I planned to go out and have some fun. But something came up that I had to deal with before I could leave, so I asked my friends to go ahead without me. I said I would join them later on because it was Christmas night and there were a lot of things to do. We had a repair point (meeting place) named Redbull at Akwa, in front of the hotel, where we were supposed to all meet at a certain time.

When I finished with the issue that held me behind, I headed to the repair point to meet everyone so we could decide where to start our fun night, but I couldn't find anybody. After hours of waiting, I found myself alone. I visited a couple of nightclubs but still could not find anybody, and since I could not waste the night by going back home, I decided instead to watch a movie.

I looked for the closest movie theater, and I bought a ticket. I did not even look to see what movie was playing. I went in and got a seat, and I was like ten minutes late into the movie, but I did not care because I wanted to kill some time. I enjoyed the movie about a good man accompanied by twelve other men, healing sick people, opening the eyes of the blind, changing water into wine, and teaching life-changing messages. He got captured by some religious leaders, who accused him of something I could not understand, and he was beaten for no apparent reason.

I felt compassionate, and I sympathized with the man, and I started to cry like a little boy. I believed he didn't deserve that type of treatment. It was so painful to watch the man being tortured that I decided to get out and go home without finishing the movie.

I was still crying on my way home. It was the first time I saw the movie Jesus of Nazareth, and I was not smart enough to find out who the guy in the movie was. Maybe because it was not the time for me to meet the Lord, and I did not know that the man in the movie was God, but somebody would tell me later it was Jesus, the son of God, who came to die for our sins.

At the time, not knowing the gospel of Christ, I always envisioned God as a supreme being who nobody could touch, not even angels, and learning He was the one getting a beating in the movie was inconceivable to me. I did not know that, to save me, He had to give His life for mine.

I thank God because He would, later on, open my eyes and make me see His love through His suffering on the cross. This event was a seed of the life, promise, and deliverance to come, and the plan He had to bless me before I was even conceived in my mother's womb, much like Joseph.

CHAPTER 5

Education

The school environment in Douala was not suitable for learning, and this would explain my multiple repeated grades. I was not good in school because my parents could not help with my homework, and I was psychologically and emotionally damaged through a series of perpetuated abuses that lasted until my adult life.

I was not just abused at home; I was also abused at school because of my slow learning process. School abuse traumatized me as well as home abuse because I was often subjected to many types of punishment, including being beaten with a whip, which I still have the scars from.

In eighth grade, I had a teacher named Carlos, who abused me more than any other teacher. Early in the morning, he would give a writing test, and I would be

Someone knew I needed help to unlock whatever was preventing me from being successful in school because I would later need whatever certificate I would obtain to go to the United States of America.

I moved from Douala to a city called Bangangte in 1989 to live with my uncle, and that was how I met Jenette. My life completely changed during the one year I spent there. I attended a school named Sainte Veuve of Bangangte, approximately four miles from our residence. Bangangte is in the western region of the country, about 150 km from Douala—the economic capital—and about 265 km from Yaoundé—the political capital. Its estimated population is approximately 40,000, and its climate ranges between 14 to 22 Celsius at night and between 24 to 30 Celsius during the day.

This was not the first time my mom made me change cities and schools. I moved to Bazou in 1982 for my final year in elementary school because of the many cases of abuse I was subjected to by several teachers.

I met a teacher who was so savvy in math that he was able to help me break down all the learning barriers I had in math. The issue I had in math was that I could not differentiate or attribute a sign to a number. He taught me that the sign of a number was the one that precedes the number, and every number had a sign even when you did not see one. This revelation unlocked all my issues.

I guessed my previous teachers did not quite explain how signs were attributed to numbers in a way I could have understood. They were only interested in beating and making fun of me.

I thanked the Lord for the Bangangte teacher who broke it down for me. Since math had a universal language, it did not require grammar, and everybody could understand it, so I put all my effort into math. This would help me be successful through ninth grade to my thirteenth grade and forward. I successfully completed my eighth-grade year after repeating it. The Lord, behind the scenes, purposely sent me to Bangangte to resolve my educational issue, which would be of great importance in God's plan for my life.

At the end of 1989, I returned to Douala to start the ninth grade, and from there on, I never repeated a grade. I successfully completed the ninth grade, which was capped by an exam called CPA, which stands for Certificate of Professional Aptitude. I successfully passed to go to tenth grade.

Tenth grade was the beginning of high school. My high school was very far from our house, and I had to walk at least seven miles one way to school because there were no school buses.

I would think that after spending a year far away from my dad, our relationship would be better once I came back home, but it was not. On the contrary, my relationship with my dad worsened to the point where he did not want to see me around him anymore, and he kicked me out of the house.

By God's grace, I had a neighbor, Mr. Innocent, who had followed my family abuse story for years. As soon as he heard that I had been kicked out of our house, he called me and gave me a place to stay.

Now, I was a member of Mr. Innocent's family, and my dad did not like it because he believed that Mr. Innocent had challenged him, and a cool war began between the two of them. Mr. Innocent became a father to me and took care of me as his own. He provided me with a stable home, and I believed the Lord was watching over me all along. Mr. Innocent was a big leader of a company, and he made sure that during the summer break of the following year, I had a paid internship to help me cover my high school expenses.

The three months of internship helped me with my school tuition and other personal expenses. Mr. Innocent was a providence from the Lord. He would later tell me he liked me for what I had accomplished so far. I graduated from middle technical school in a field that was very difficult—the electronic/electrical field—in order to start technical high school. The challenging field had fewer graduates than any other technical field in the entire country.

I graduated high school. The graduation rate was one out of the thousand people taking the exam. Even though my dad did not want me around, he was proud of me when I graduated from high school.

My favorite subjects in school were math, physics, and science, which would later help me join the United States military. Mr. Innocent helped me, through his hospitality, to complete my high school years. To graduate middle and high technical school in Cameroon required passing national exams, and it was a big deal. Exam results were announced through the national radio, and the entire country was on alert the day of the results.

The exam promulgation was and may still be a very stressful event because, one way or another, everyone in the neighborhood would know if you passed or not. I worked very hard, and my name was always on the passing list and called on the radio. I felt a sense of pride because all the neighbors talked about my success. I had successfully passed all my three exams once without repeating any exam, which was very difficult to achieve in my field of study. Somehow, people saw me through a different lens, not like a stupid kid, but the smartest one. The Lord started to restore my name.

There were three exams everyone in my field had to complete to successfully pass the certification exam. The Certificate of Professional Aptitude is administered in tenth grade. The Probationary Technician Certificate was administered in twelfth grade, and the Baccalaureate of Technical Secondary Education was administered in thirteenth grade in the French education system. All exams were administered by the secondary education ministry, and they were all high-stake and mandatory examinations certified completion of lower-secondary and upper-secondary vocational education programs.

The Probationary Technician Certificate was a requirement for students wishing to move forward to the Baccalaureate of Technical Secondary Education. Some students spent years in the twelfth grade trying to pass the Probationary Technician Certificate because the certificate was your passport to move on to the thirteenth grade, and a lot of students gave up at that grade level after many unsuccessful attempts to pass the exam. Those who made it to the thirteenth grade sometimes gave up as well because they could not pass the thirteenth-grade exam. Or, since it was a two-part exam, they may have passed the writing part but failed the technical part. You could easily find a twenty-five-year-old student in the twelfth grade.

I obtained my Probationary Technician Certificate and my Baccalaureate of Secondary Education when I was still living with Mr. Innocent. It was important to get those certificates, even though I did not know that it would later help me satisfy the requirement to go to the United States of America.

So God's plan for my life started a little earlier than I had thought. I also believed that God wanted me to play a part in His plan for my life by completing high school, without which I could not have traveled to the United States of America.

Almost a year after I graduated from high school, my dad called me back home. I had made him so proud by being the only one passing my Baccalaureate of Secondary Education in the neighborhood, but I conditioned my return. I asked him to give me a piece of land near our family house so I could build my own apartment to guarantee my security. There was no trust between the two of us, and the apartment would be mine. My dad agreed.

I loved my dad, even though he brought me through difficult times, and there is no greater love than the love of a father. Being away, being loved by someone else, and being well taken care of by someone else did not replace my father and his love. I always longed for my dad's love. I did not enjoy my childhood and adolescence the way I should have. I believed my adolescence was taken away from me because I used to see other boys and their dads holding hands on the street.

I was envious, and I kept asking myself, "Why not me?"

After I successfully completed secondary school, I went to college. I was building my one-bedroom apartment while I went to college to further my education. I used the money I had saved by doing different small jobs and internships to build my apartment.

Continuing my education was one way for me to set myself up for success in life. Completing my bachelor's would have definitely helped me accomplish my goal. At least, that was my belief, but the reality would prove otherwise.

I also wanted to be able to support my siblings and my parents once I finished with my education and got a good job. Almost at the end of my freshmen year, I realized I would not even be able to complete my first year because of the expense associated with college. I stopped going to college and focused on finishing my apartment. Everything was done by me except the roof.

After completing my apartment, I went back home with a seed of the love of Jesus in me because of a young lady called Rose. She loved Jesus and was a living example of what it meant to be a Christ-follower.

Since I stopped going to college and my apartment was completed and I had moved in, I focused only on finding a job. I soon realized the reality of looking for a job in Cameroon. It was not easy because I could not find a job in that corrupt system.

Since I could not find a permanent job, I started doing little side jobs as an electrician and as a block layer to survive. But the author of hope was making a route into my life as He did for Joseph.

CHAPTER 6

Believer

In college, I thought I knew it all. A Jehovah's Witness used to come by our house to talk about Jehovah, and I used my intellect to convince him that God's story was a myth, and even if God's story was real, He was not a fair God. I pointed out inequality, suffering, and human wickedness.

I found most of his responses unsatisfactory. I was one of those people whose gospel preaching did not have any effect because I was hurt, coupled with the fact that many Christians I knew were not living up to their preaching. Nothing was going to change my perception of Christianity except God Himself.

God's love was very strong. It would later break any barrier and any unbelief I had. He used the life of a young lady to do that.

My life changed when I moved in with Innocent. Rose was twenty-four years old, and we were friends. She was related to Mr. Innocent's wife, Mrs. Suzanne. She was beautiful and an independent woman. She was the type of girl any young guy wanted to go out with, including me, but she was out of my league.

Rose, before she knew the Lord, was sexually promiscuous. She got saved and became a different woman, and she also became a devout churchgoer. Remember God will use any means to accomplish His plan for our life.

Because of my dad's kicking me out of the house after an argument, I found myself living under the same roof as Rose. I noticed a radical change in her. I knew her past very well, and I knew the type of life she had lived before. The boyfriend traffic had stopped, and she was free from immorality, especially of a sexual nature. Nightclubs were no longer part of her practice. She became very polite, and she even did my laundry when I was living with her.

She preached the gospel to me, but I was quick to shut her down, as I did with the Jehovah's Witness guy. But she would not give up on me. She wasn't pushy and never tried to get me to change my position. Her goal instead was to be instrumental in demonstrating a relationship with God. I saw in her a deep, perceptible love and a real personal connection to Jesus Christ. She brought to light some of the answers to my questions by showing me the love of Jesus.

When she asked me if I had a personal relationship with God, I truly had no idea what she was talking about, so I did not know how to answer her question. It's easy to fool ourselves into believing we are a child of God when we're not questioned about our faith. We may not know the depth of what we're missing.

I became curious to know and understand what she was talking about, so I accepted her invitation to visit her church. To tell you the truth, Rose was able to help me prepare my heart by the way she lived. I was ready to experience the joy, peace, hope, and love that she had.

I visited Rose's church the next Sunday, and so began my conversion and a new life in Christ. The first thing which struck me was how welcoming the members were and how a community of believers was so passionate about becoming Christ-like. I also noticed that one row was reserved for men and another for women, and all women had head coverings (I personally believe the covering is no longer relevant).

The pastor of the church was Pastor Dagwe, from whom I received my very first message.

The message was life-changing. At one point, I thought Rose had laid down my life story to the pastor in advance because everything in the message felt directed to me. The message was about fornication, liars, theft, idols, forgiveness, and more.

One of the texts used by the pastor was Matthew 15:19 (NKJV): "For out of the heart proceed evil thoughts, murders, adulteries, fornications, thefts, false witness, and blasphemies." I remember the message like it was preached yesterday because I had my first real encounter with Jesus that Sunday.

After the message, the pastor asked for people who wanted to give their life to Jesus to come forward. I defied my fear to be the first one in front of the pulpit. The pastor led us through a repentance and acceptance prayer. I met Jesus. Jesus is not like the marabouts, who always tell people that their problems are caused by other people. Jesus told me I was my one problem because I was not living a righteous life. He was ready to bless and change my story and make me a new person if I trusted Him.

I left the church changed and ready to make some dramatic decisions in my life. My first six resolutions were:

First: Stop stealing from my parents, especially from my mom. I could not mess with my dad's money anyway because I remembered one episode where I stole 100 FCFA (around 0.20 cents) from Dad to buy a chocolate bar, and my dad found out. He came to my school, and he almost killed me in front of my classmates by beating me up with a machete.

Second: Stop fornicating. I broke up with my girlfriend and explained to her I was a new person. She didn't quite understand what was going on with me until later when she became a child of God as well. My decision left her wondering, and she decided to find out about Jesus, and the Lord got her in the process.

Third: Stay away from idols. I also let my parents know I would no longer participate in the skull ritual because I had found the blameless Lamb of God, the perfect sacrifice of God, who gave His life for you and me, and He shared His blood on the cross, so we do not have to sacrifice any animals to the dead anymore. My parents called me a disgrace to the family, and that was the beginning of my persecution. I was resolute to stay firm.

Fourth: Forgive as I assessed all the painful abuses I went through during my childhood and adolescence by friends and family. I dealt with the effects of childhood maltreatment, which were linked to my physical, psychological, and behavioral problems. I also had to deal with chronic low self-esteem, severe dissociative states, and poor peer relations.

Fifth: Stop smoking and drinking. I needed God's grace. The Lord says in 1 Corinthians 3:17 (NASB), "If any man destroys the temple of God, God will destroy him,

for the temple of God is holy, and that is what you are."
I am the temple of God, and I must do my best to give
a clean, pure, holy living space for my God to dwell in.
I'm not saying smoking or drinking are sins because the
Bible doesn't say. It's everyone's choice to make.

Last, I decided to know the truth and put to rest the
feud between my mom and my uncle and reconcile the
two. I went to my mom and asked her why she was no
longer speaking to her brother. She repeated the story
she once told years ago. My uncle mysteriously managed to kill my little sister two hundred miles away
from Douala, where he was living, even though a different car and driver were identified at the scene of the
accident—my mom's brother-in-law. My uncle was not
aware of the accusation because it was all done behind
the scenes by my mom and her siblings. So I asked my
mom to confront my uncle and asked if he was the person, and she said she was not ready to confront him. I
mentioned to her that years had passed since she had
spoken with her brother, and it was not normal.

Since my mother stopped speaking to her older brother, who had acted as a father to her, I had no
choice but to be the peacemaker with God's grace. So I
visited my uncle against my mother's wishes. My uncle
was very surprised to see me and commented on my
growth.

He invited me to sit down and asked about the surprise visit. I told him I had stuff in my heart I had carried for years, and I was dying to ask him about it. He told me he had a feeling something was wrong because we had not visited him for years. So I went straight to the point and asked him if he was behind my little sister's accident and death, and I told him my mom was accusing him of killing her little baby. He checked his head and put it into his hand and almost cried.

What kind of nonsense was this? I stayed quiet because I did not know what to say.

It was odd—a little sister accusing her big brother of killing her child.

Finally, he lifted his head. "How did your mom come up with the conclusion?"

"The marabout. According to your sister, after her little girl died, she went to consult a marabout to find out who was behind the killing, and the marabout pointed the finger at a family member who had a white car. You were the only person with a white car in the family, so she concluded it was you."

"Let's go!" My uncle headed for the door.

We took his car and went to see my mom. When we got home, my mom was surprised to see us, and I told her it was time for the truth.

My uncle wasted no time. "Why are you accusing me of the death of your daughter after everything I have done for you?"

It was fun to watch. They spoke, and my uncle could not believe my mom and her siblings were accusing him, and they did not have the guts to confront him. At a certain point, my mom knew she was wrong about her brother. Mom rescinded the marabout, but it took them years to repair their relationship.

I held bitterness toward a lot of wrong deeds done against me. I did not believe it would be healthy for me to carry those pains into my new life with Christ. I forgave my dad and many other people who were jerks to me. I felt free.

After more than four months in the faith, I got baptized. I felt a transformative power over me, and I witnessed one of the girls in my group get baptized with the Holy Spirit. I could hear her speaking in tongues. God manifested Himself three feet away from me. This was a life-changing experience for me, and it strengthened my faith. I still have the image of the event in my mind. I took my baptism very seriously. I decided to surrender my flesh and rise in spirit with the Lord as one.

My parents were not so appreciative of me changing my religion from ancestor worship to Jesus Christ worship, especially my dad. Jesus said in Luke 4:8 (ESV), "It is written, 'you shall worship the Lord your God, and him only shall you serve.'" I was indeed a new creation because I knew and still know my new birthday in Christ.

Second Corinthians 5:17 (NIV) states, "Therefore, if anyone is in Christ, he is a new creation; the old has gone, the new has come."

A little history about my previous church. The inside of the church was divided into two rows of the sitting bench. One was for women, and the other was for men, and every single woman in the church had a head covering on. The churches had one pastor, two elders, and some deacons. And the two elders had different personalities; one was very strict on how to behave and live a Christ-like life, and the other was very passive and calm and could tolerate some behaviors that were not sinful in nature, like letting men and women sit together in the church. The strict elder's name was Mr. Johnson, and the passive elder's name was Mr. Kue.

They were complementary to each other and served the church very well. For example, we used to dance during praise and worship service, and Elder Johnson told us we ought to dance like Christians, not like nonbelievers. Even though there's not a biblical or a Christian way to dance, we always obeyed and danced to his satisfaction.

I believe there are always miracles in obedience. Jesus asked Peter to cast his net on the other side of the boat, and his obedience produced the miracle of an abundance of fish. Through obedience to His word, my life was a miraculous change for good. It was through obedience that Moses had stretched out his hands over the Red Sea to experience deliverance, and it was through obedience that the blind man washed his eyes in the pool before he gained sight.

Church members were subject to a lot of restrictions. For example, they asked women in the church not to wear shorts because men would see their thighs, to always wear a decent dress that would not expose any part of their body. We always chose to obey because we knew they could never ask us to do something sinful in nature because they loved the Lord.

Elder Johnson did not care about hurting anyone's feelings. All he cared about was preaching the truth of the word of God. On the other hand, Elder Kue cared about people's feelings, but he was still successful in getting his message across without compromising the truth. Both were very loved by the members of the church because we knew they meant well, and we knew they loved the congregation. They were very active in the church and in each member's life, and they were like a father to most of us.

They taught us how to love Christ, and both were an example to follow because they lived and practiced what they preached. I personally visited each elder a lot for advice, and I did not have to schedule an appointment to do so because both had an open-door policy for members. Their contribution made me the man of faith I am today.

They did not just make me a man of faith but a strong disciple anchored into the word of God, who can stand the strong winds of adversity. Winds will always blow in life, and temptation will always happen. How I choose to deal with it is measured by how deeply connected I am with the Lord Jesus.

The Lord said in 1 Corinthians 10:13 (NIV), "No temptation has overtaken you except what is common to mankind. And God is faithful; he will not let you be tempted beyond what you can bear. But when you are tempted, he will also provide a way out so you can endure it."

It was true! I was able to stand most of the trials and windblown at me in the context of poverty and culture in Cameroon. In the US, I would not have the same spiritual support I had back home, and this would negatively impact my spiritual life in a different context and culture.

Both elders were called radical because they were like the first-century followers of Christ. They were radical in their preaching, especially Elder Johnson, and they wanted us to follow the Scripture to a tee. They were very strict on how to conduct the business of the Lord.

Together, they were the founding fathers of the Airport Apostolic Church, and their teaching came from the entire Bible.

I sometimes felt like I was still under the law. For example, women were not authorized to wear men's clothes. This teaching came from Deuteronomy 22:5 (NIV), "A woman must not wear men's clothing, nor a man wear women's clothing, for the Lord your God detests anyone who does this." But it was under the law, and we are now under grace. Dating, politics, and marrying a non-believer were all prohibited. I believed they did everything through the love of God, even though some of those radical teachings were not always right or biblical, but their teaching gave me a good foundation in Christ.

Bible study was conducted by Elder Johnson. (Peace to his soul. He passed away in February 2021.) They both conducted the new convert meetings, and they had a gift of teaching and transmitting knowledge to others. They would break down the Bible to the level everyone could understand, and they focused on the transformative life the Holy Spirit could help one achieve if we let Him guide our life.

Elder Johnson would tell us about sins one could commit without the chance to think about them and those we had the time, room, and space to think about before we committed them.

One of the teachings of Elder Johnson still sticks in my mind, more than twenty years later. He helped me withstand fornication's temptation in my life. He gave an example of a young man and a young woman calling themselves Christians, who were dating, and thinking about having sex.

He said, "For a Christian child of God, the Holy Spirit will always be there to help or warn us when we are tempted. For instance, if you are thinking about having sex when you are not married, the Holy Spirit will warn you about fornication, which is a sin, and He will advise you to keep your body pure until you get married."

He also said, "Since the Holy Spirit is very gentle and persistent, He will warn you every step of the way. If you decide to move forward and have sex, and you meet with your partner, the Holy Spirit will warn you. When you decide to remove your clothes and lie down on the bed, the Holy Spirit again warns you, and before you take final action to consummate the sin, the Holy Spirit is still there to warn you. The Holy Spirit warns you again and again, but you can choose to disobey."

This is true for any type of temptation we go through as a child of God, and He is always there to help.

I would need to write a completely separate book for all of his examples. It is true that God is always a step away to help. It is up to me to follow His instruction in troubled times or when facing temptation and when other issues arise on my walk with Jesus.

The Holy Spirit is God Himself, and He came and dwelled in me once I gave Him my life and decided to follow Christ to make me a new person. It is the soft voice in me, helping me make the correct, right, and holy choice so the whole me can be kept blameless. When He came to take me with Him, and He was a sensible person who was easily quenched when I decided not to listen to Him or obey Him.

One of the jobs of the Holy Spirit was to motivate and regenerate my heart to live in obedience to God. "But the Advocate, the Holy Spirit, whom the Father will send in my name, will teach you all things and will remind you of everything I have said to you" (John 14:26, NIV).

I would later feel like this message of life's abstention from fornication was a little too late. After the Lord had forgiven me for all my sins, and I had forgotten most of them, but fornication or any sexual relationship I had before knowing the Lord still had a crimson hold on me. I still felt somehow connected to the past relationships, even though I did not have any desire to do anything with them. They still occupied a part of my mind, especially those I had a strong bond with and with whom I had made some promise.

I remember one particular girl I made an alliance of blood with. She and I used a little sharp blade to cut our fingers and drank each other's blood. We were naïve, but the enemy used it for years to make my life miserable. I thanked God for His grace because the Lord would help me deal and get out of the vow to free me to be the man I am to Rachel, my wife. But it required a lot of spiritual battles from me.

I often wonder how people without Christ fight this type of battle. All of it could have been prevented if I had not engaged in fornication. The consequence of this sin that I would suffer later in life was true for any other command of God I did not obey. It made me realize that the Word of God is like a loving and protecting letter to His children because I did not feel love when I was hurt.

Even today, I notice that some Christians do not believe abstention is possible. I gave my life to the Lord and abstained from myself for years until I got married to my beautiful wife, Rachel. Regardless of what our society says, it is important to remember that God has called each person, male and female, to live in purity and in holiness. First Thessalonians 4:3 and 7 (The Voice) says, "Now this is God's will for you: set yourselves apart and live holy lives; avoid polluting yourselves with sexual defilement... For God did not call us to be impure but to live holy lives."

Elder Johnson and Elder Kue were involved and present in everything we did, evangelization, youth program, and youth convention.

I walked about six miles every Sunday to attend the church service, which was rich in praise, worship, and the word of the Lord. The church's leader always let the worshipping service be led by the Holy Spirit, and sometimes we could worship for hours. We could feel the presence of God in our midst.

After the worship was over, the pastor or someone else who had been designated would pass down some announcements for the week ahead. If there was something that needed prayer, we would do so after the announcement; then, the pastor would go straight to the Word of God.

I always entered the church with excitement and reverence to the authority of God, as if I was going to see an important person, like a president. I always made sure I gave my devout attention to listening to the word of God when it was preached. It did not matter which channel it was coming through.

The service sometimes could have gone up to three hours, but we did not care because the love of being together in fellowship outweighed any other program in our life. After the service was over, we still could not depart from each other, and we went to members' house after house, and I would get back home sometimes late in the evening.

The two elders were good shepherds, and I would always honor them. I vividly remember their moral rectitude, their unwavering commitment to God, and their uncompromising messages. Their personalities in Christ inspired me to want to follow Jesus. The church congregation was blessed with those two men of God, and it was also blessed with prophets, prophetesses, and deacons—like Deacon Mado, who was a woman of prayer and a pastor. They all played a vital role in my growth with the Lord Jesus.

We were always looking out for each other. Other than Sunday, we visited each other, and the subject of our discussion was nothing but Jesus Christ. We were fans of nothing else but the Lord Jesus, and this helped us to be in the presence of God all the time. It did not matter how much money we had; we were living in heaven on earth.

We had a dynamic circle of young believers that was always looking out for each other, and many of them would play a great role in my life's story, which is similar to Joseph's story.

CHAPTER 7

Believer, God's Promise, and Miracle Reconciliation

I was a changed man by the time I moved from Mr. Innocent's house to my new apartment. My parents did not approve of my going to a church other than the Catholic church because, even though they were not Catholic, it was considered safer in many prospects than other Christian churches. But they started to see a change in my behavior.

After many persecutions, such as disownment, they noticed I would not leave Jesus to go back to my old beliefs or to the Catholic church. But instead, my mom and my dad saw a new person in me, and they began to accept my decision to worship Jesus. They noticed I was respectful with no more girlfriends; they also noticed that I had cut all ties with friends that were negatively impacting me. I lived a life of abstinence and honored them as my parents by respecting, listening, and obeying them. I did whatever they wanted me to do, except worship the skull.

All my neighbors noticed a change in my life as well. I preached the gospel like the Samaritan woman at the well, who went to those who had gossiped about her. In the process, I lost a lot of friends, and people thought that I, like Rose, had lost my mind.

Over the years, my relationship with my dad had been tense, and we never had the son-and-dad relationship I desired. Giving my life to the Lord was the turning point of our relationship.

My dad and I started to be very close, which was a miracle. We all need a good relationship with our parents, with significant others, with our children, and with neighbors because it is important for our souls. I was very miserable without my dad's love. Christ broke the curse between my dad and me, and we became good friends. I started to know my dad and what kind of man he was and where he was coming from.

For the first time, my dad told me about his family background, his parents, what he had gone through as a child, and how it affected him. All this conversation took place in my new one-bedroom apartment. Also, my dad was no longer a heavy drinker. In the first two years that I was a child of God, a lot more changed between my dad and me than in my entire childhood and adolescent life. I continued to build a healthy habit by reading my Bible and making time with God. It helped me change the way I thought about life.

My past skull cult culture helped me understand the Lord's sacrifice on the cross because it was all about animal sacrifice. With the Lord Jesus' ultimate sacrifice on the cross, I would no longer have to sacrifice animals for the forgiveness of my sins.

I was passionate to know Christ and apply His word to every area of my life. I try to keep Jesus at the center of my life. So, through my relationship with the Lord, my faith was deepened and, in many ways, awakened. There was no more fighting between my dad and me; on the contrary, love took precedence over fear and hatred. I became very active in the church, and I participated in every Bible study and prayer session.

The fellowship of the brotherhood was incredible. My new friends were children of God. We shared the same values and love for Jesus Christ. We helped each other out, and we shared meals together. We also shared our problems and our challenges together, and we became a very strong family bound by the love of God.

We had Bible study every Wednesday, prayed every Thursday, and went out for evangelization every Saturday. Everything I did going forward involved the Lord.

Actually, in the book of Matthew 12:48-50 (NIV), the Lord replied to whoever wanted to know who Jesus' brothers and sisters were, "'Who is my mother, and who are my brothers?' Pointing to his disciples, he said, 'Here are my mother and my brothers. For whoever does the will of my Father in heaven is my brother and sister and mother.'"

Some of us children of God did not grasp the concept of family. One thing we ignored was that if we believed in Christ and our biological child would not believe, each of us could end up in a different place. This is a sad reality and why it is very important to introduce the Lord to our children.

I felt love, and I also felt a sense of belonging to my new family. Our communion drove us to be better and to watch over each other. I was convinced of the Lord's love for me.

I remembered a profound scene I had with church members when I returned after a few months of absence from the church. I had left the church for six months because the Lord had opened a door for temporary employment with a sub-contractor working on the pipeline project. The pipeline was going to transport oil from Chad to Cameroon and then by sea to Europe.

After six months, I came back, and when I entered the church, everybody got up to hug me. I felt love, a feeling I had never had before in my entire life, and I knew I was in the right place.

I could feel God's presence around and could not go a day without praising and worshipping the Lord for what He had done for me on the cross to prove He loved me. This gave a reason to my heart to always turn to and depend on Him.

Reading the Bible was very important to me as a child of God. It helped me grow, and it edified me as well. The Lord's Word was written on my heart, and I knew the Holy Spirit would bring forward those words to save me from any situation.

For example, I was once able to get out of a life-threatening circumstance in which the tension was high. The Holy Spirit reminded me of a Bible verse suited for the situation.

Our family home was surrounded by apartments, and one of the tenants whom we considered as family lost a beautiful baby girl. It was very sad for us because we all loved the little girl.

One day, we all gathered for a memorial service to mourn her, and to my surprise, I overheard someone close to the family of the deceased spreading a rumor about my dad being responsible for the death of the little girl.

I was infuriated and devastated. As a child of God, I approached the father to find out if he knew anything about the rumor. The girl's dad was a very calm man, but as I was speaking with him, the girl's uncle jumped into our conversation and became very aggressive. He started to throw punches, yelling that my dad had killed their girl.

The culture in Cameroon is to believe that nobody dies from natural causes—someone is always responsible for a death (marabout 101). But the spirit of God came to my rescue by reminding me of Proverbs 17:14 (NIV), "The beginning of strife is like letting out water, so quit before the quarrel breaks out."

I listened to the Holy Spirit and stopped myself, then fled the scene. I concluded that this was the result of having the word of God anchored in me. Also, in John 14:26 (NIV), "But the Advocate, the Holy Spirit, whom the Father will send in my name, will teach you all things and will remind you of everything I have said to you."

I found out that there are always profound and miraculous reasons behind our obedience to God's Word that we cannot see at the present time.

I am not saying I had everything under control, and I was far from being perfect. Reading my Bible and putting it into practice was the cornerstone of my faithful life and my walk with Jesus. I believed that those who are faithful with God's business attracted God's love, which could manifest itself as a blessing, love, protection, and more.

But I would become a different kind of believer when I got to the US. I would become complacent with what I had and stop reading my Bible as a daily routine. You do not need to move to a healthy place like I did to become complacent or backslide from the love of God because it can happen in our own backyard. When we find ourselves complacent, we start to lose our first love with the Lord, especially when everything is going well in our life. One thing we all have in common is that we tend to go to Him when we become uncomfortable.

My previous church was built in 1987 with temporary building material (wood), and it had been seriously damaged. The church leadership decided to rebuild the church, but this time with concrete block material. The designing, planning, and construction were all done by church members, and I was involved in the construction process since I was not employed at that time.

I participated by doing all the electrical work because I was an electrician. I assisted in any capacity I could, like laying concrete blocks and mixing mortar.

There were three of us—Marcel, Jean, and me—who were seen as heroes because we took the church construction seriously by showing up every day to assist. We dedicated our time as much as we could, and through our faithfulness, God promised to bless us through a prophecy given in the church. The prophecy was clear, and it was about blessing us by making us travel out of the country to a country with milk and honey.

The three of us took the promise of God to heart, and we knew it would come to pass.

There was no salary involved in our church construction, and we all worked as volunteers for the love of Jesus. We were determined to serve the Lord in any capacity possible. We built the church from the ground up, and the three of us were tremendously blessed by the Lord by leaving the country as God promised.

Marcel and I immigrated to the US, and Jean went to France by the grace of our Lord. The Lord used a prophecy to give me a heads-up about His plan for my life, just like He used a dream to give a heads-up to Joseph. But just like Joseph, I did not know how all this would unfold. Like Joseph's brothers did not believe his dream, I had brothers who did not believe God would do something of that magnitude in my life.

CHAPTER 8

Social Economic

Cameroon suffered from a lot of factors which made the country not a good place to live and do business. For example, stagnant per capita income, inequitable distribution of Cameroon's wealth, confiscation of power by some elites, a corrupt justice system, continuing impunity for embezzlement of public funds, weak and corrupt governance, and in general, a corrupt climate for business. Those endemic situations made it difficult for a regular citizen to find a job and make a living.

The Cameroonian government was aware of the situation and put in place a mechanism to fight corruption, but there is still a lot to do. Even in the bad living conditions and in a bad economy, my mom did her best to send me to vocational school because she believed it would at least guarantee me employment as soon as I graduated.

My family needed me to find a job to help, and my technical training should have been enough for me to find suitable employment. But I was ignorant of the corrupt environment. I did not imagine how hard it would be to get a job. Obtaining a job in Cameroon was like trying to put a camel through the eye of a needle.

I started each day by visiting my mom at her place of business. I begged for 100 FCFA (0.20 cents in the US) to get something to eat, especially when we did not have any leftover food in the house.

After I ate, I headed on my journey to look for a job. I did not have any internet access. I remember walking fifteen to twenty miles a day, going to different companies to submit job applications. My naïve understanding of the employment practice in Cameroon caused me a lot of pain and suffering. When I would later apply for a job in the US, in most cases, they would ask for my skills. In Cameroon, they asked me who I knew because employment was not based on merits or skills but on who you knew.

So discrimination in the labor market was a problem in Cameroon. I did not know a company CEO, company manager, or any member of the government to help me to find a job. Mr. Innocent's company had gone out of business, and he could no longer help me. Most young people today are in the same position I was in years ago, and a lot of them are very educated with bachelor's, master's, and PhDs.

Unfortunately, unemployment is a serious problem in Cameroon, which creates poverty and a low standard of living. The lack of a creative economy—where Cameroonians could develop careers through the arts, media, and design—green jobs, sports, a fair justice system, value addition for natural resources, and eco-tourism played a role in the underdevelopment of the economy and young Cameroonian unemployment.

Since I did not have anyone to help me with my employment problem, my flesh came out with a worldly solution, which was to join the political party in power. So I joined to get close to decision-makers and elites. People used the party in power as a channel to get a job. The unemployed are still doing this today.

I militated in the political party in power for some years, and I made my way up to becoming a youth base committee president. It got me close to our neighborhood base committee president, whom I knew very well. I was quick to talk to him about my employment problem. He introduced me to the president of the subsection, a businesswoman named Madame Esther. I became very close to her. I visited her at her house at any time of the day.

One day, I introduced my problem to her, and she agreed to help me find a job. I was so happy I would finally find a job—at least, that was my belief. She recommended me to multiple public companies' CEOs by writing recommendation letters for employment opportunities. I was very good at following those recommendations by calling the CEO's secretary to follow up, but I had no positive answers.

After a while, my joy faded, and I lost confidence that I would find employment through her multiple recommendations.

Since her recommendations would not yield any fruit, I decided to change my strategy by focusing on the biggest target, which was the political party's section president. Today he's a minister and a member of the government. Back then, the minister was the section president of the department of Douala 11 (the equivalent of a county in the US). He was able to meet and connect to any members of the government.

So I brought the problem to my base president's attention again, to see the section president to solicit his help. He agreed to help me meet with the section's president as he had with the subsection president, Mrs. Esther. I tried multiple times to get in touch with our section president by phone but never got the chance to speak with him. We also visited his home in the hope that we might catch him.

Our efforts were in vain, and I was back to square one. I was determined to find a job, and I looked for help everywhere. It was true that I was also praying, but not as I should have because I mostly counted on my ability to make it happen.

But I was trusting in men to help me find a job instead of looking to heaven, where my help always comes from. At one point in my life, I felt I could have accepted a job even from the devil himself, but I thanked the Lord because I was obedient even in my life's challenges.

When I lose my grip on hope, my lovely Father in heaven reminds me not to put my hope in a man but in Him alone. The word of God says in Psalm 146:3 (NIV), "Do not put your trust in princes, in mortal men, who cannot save." One thing I did not know was that He saw my desperation, and He was working behind the scenes like He always does to bless me with a miracle job.

In my desperation, I remembered a message Pastor Dagwe had preached, "It is very difficult to be the light of the world and be an active politician because it is almost impossible to mix water with oil."

I was not a politician, just someone looking for a job, but I compromised a lot in the process as I was playing politics to get a job.

I have a lot of respect for all pastors, and I was good friends with my pastor back then. He had an open-door policy when it came to visits or counseling. After he learned of my involvement with a political party, he brought it up during one of our conversations and reminded me that water and oil do not mix. I learned how it was very difficult for me as a politician to love politics and love God at the same time because politics almost took precedence over my love for Jesus. I believed that politics and God were just like money and God in the Bible, where you could only serve one master. From my own experience, politicians would surely compromise their faith, and they would surely make a fool of themselves. Few are able to manage both, but they have to put a priority on Jesus and nothing else. Compromises like lies and distortion of facts became a common practice.

Unemployment in Cameroon had driven many young citizens to commit unbelievable sins to survive in a corrupt culture where the weak were powerless against a system working against them. The corrupt system affected every single section of life, and it worked against almost every Cameroonian.

For example, according to Heritage.org:

> Property rights are recognized by law, but Cameroon's weak judiciary makes enforcement sporadic, and land disputes are common. The inefficient judicial system is also vulnerable to political interference. Corruption and cronyism are systemic, and demands

for bribes, from gaining school admission to fixing traffic infractions, are common. Revenues from oil and mineral extractions are not openly reported. Enforcement of anti-corruption statutes targets political opponents.

According to the World Bank:

Cameroon suffers from weak governance, hindering its development and ability to attract investment. It ranks 152 out of 180 countries in the 2018 Transparency International Corruption Perceptions Index, and 166 out of 190 economies in the World Bank's Doing Business 2019 report.

Borgenproject.org also stated, "Despite being an independent country from 1960, Cameroon still has an autocratic ruler who made the country one of the poorest in the world. The country has a lot of work to do, especially in the fields of child labor and corruption."

I graduated from technical school in 1994 and looked for a job for six years, but I could not find any. In 2000, the government started recruiting military personnel again. The Lord did not have any issue about how I went to find a job, but with how the process was making me compromise His love for me. But repentance, God's love, and grace restored my peace and joy.

The Lord who raised Joseph to the status of a prime minister was also working to raise me in status.

CHAPTER 9

Joining Cameroon's Military

Because of the recession, the Cameroon government put recruitment in the military on hold for years, but this changed in 2000 and was a one-time opportunity for me. With a lot of young unemployed people, there were two types of candidates: one wanted to join because he loved the service, and one wanted to get out of their parents' house. In my case, I was both, but I really loved the military because I wanted to defend my country against foreign and domestic enemies.

You would think I would have learned from my previous mistake of not taking the time to ask God's will as I jumped into politics. But in this case, also, I was drawn in by the opportunity, not God's will.

I met all the requirements to join the military except that I was twenty-seven and the age limit was twenty-two. This could have been a red flag for me to stop right there.

Since I believed that anything was possible in Cameroon at the time, I thought the five-year age difference could be waived if I knew a high-ranking military person. When I learned about a captain through his brother Thomas, a childhood friend of mine, I asked to be introduced. I explained my situation to the captain, and he told me he would take care of things. I did not know how he would do it, but I went for it. That was how desperate I was to find a job.

Waiting on the Lord was no longer an option.

As a child of God, my faith was getting tested when it came to doing what was right, especially when I needed it so bad. I was failing that test miserably. Cameroon was and still is a very challenging country for Christians because there is corruption at all levels of business and life.

Desperation could even make a child of God do the unbelievable to survive. I was at a point where I needed a job so bad, I could bend or manipulate justice a little bit to serve my purpose. But I noticed later that the Lord was reigning in every stupid decision and made some good come out of foolishness because I learned a lot in the process.

Please, I am not asking anyone to go out there and make some foolish decision and expect God to make something out of it because it is not how it works. I was a grown man without a job, and I was still living with my parents, so I spent most of my time with my brothers in Christ. I needed to have a future to long for in my life, but it seemed like everything was out of my reach, and I had no perspective. In this situation, I just hoped age would not be an obstacle for me.

I gathered all required documents and gave them to the captain with a considerable sum of money. Every citizen had to go back to their regional capital of origin to get recruited, and my region of origin was in the west. The people living there are called Bamileke.

I was supposed to go to my capital of origin to do my physical activity and medical exam, which were all part of the recruitment process, but the captain told me not to worry about it because he would take care of it all. Naïve and eager to join the military, I believed him. He told me the man in charge of the recruitment in my region was his best friend, and they had a lot of history together. He also told me this was not the first time they had helped someone join the military with age-limit problems and without going through the normal process.

I tried to have faith in him. I knew I had put myself into this situation because I believed everything was possible in Cameroon, even joining the military without showing up to do your physical and medical exam. But this was a long stretch, and I really did have a concern and suspicion.

One had to do the required tests and exams and pledge an allegiance to serve his country before joining the military. But according to the captain, I was going to bypass these processes, and my name would magically appear in the final list of recruits. Even though I was suspicious, I had no choice or option but to continue the process because I had already given him money.

We had many situations where people were admitted to national schools which required an entry exam without taking any exam. So I thought this might be possible in the military as well. Military recruitment in Cameroon was very different from the United States recruitment process. In Cameroon, you must have a high school diploma, be physically fit, be a certain height, meet the age limit, pass medical exams, and know somebody. In contrast to the United States, where you need to have a high school diploma or a GED and to pass the ASVAB test, medical exams, and the physical activity test.

As the recruitment process was going on in each region, I had to wait and go along with the captain's plan. In the meantime, I tutored the captain's son for free to get him ready for the GED exam. He had failed after many attempts, and the captain had almost given up. I brought my expertise to help him in math since I was very knowledgeable. I cheered up the captain with money every time we met. The money I didn't have, but I was doing anything he wanted me to do because I wanted to win his favor.

I was no longer a drinker or smoker after I met the Lord, and most of the time, when I visited the captain for an update, I would find him in a bar drinking, and I would pick up the bill.

Early in the process, he presented me with a letter. According to him, the letter was sent to him by his friend, the head recruiter in my region, stating that everything was going as planned and my name was among the recruits. My fake physical exam and activities, etc., were going to be forwarded to Yaoundé, as well as those of the other recruits for final selection.

I had already spent a lot of time with the captain, and I knew his handwriting. The letter handwriting looked like his. It was the first time I thought something was not right and that I was getting played. But the Lord Jesus was in the midst of this.

After a few months, I asked him to travel to Yaoundé to follow up with my recruitment. All recruitments were completed in different cities, and all applications, physical exams, and medical exams were forwarded to Yaoundé for final selection. They did not tell you how you did or if you were selected after you finished all the different activities, but they sent the recruit's documentation to Yaoundé.

Yaoundé was the political capital where all games were played. He said yes, he would go to Yaoundé, so I gave him money for transportation. The plan was for the captain to go to the minister of defense to make sure my name would be on the final list. He was going to spend the day at the Minister of Defense Department and come back the next afternoon.

Since I suspected foul play, I went home with a plan to go back to the captain's house early the next morning to make sure he had actually traveled. When I did, I found him at home—he did not go anywhere.

I was getting screwed over by the captain.

He looked surprised to see me. The explanation I got from him was that he chose to call the minister of defense instead of traveling to make sure my name was on the final list. He said he was able to talk to the minister, who confirmed that my name was on the list.

When the captain lied to me about going to Yaoundé, I concluded that I was getting played. But I had no choice but to hang in there to the finish line.

The result finally came out, and it was the time for the truth. All selection was done in Yaoundé, and the final list of recruit candidates' names was sent to each regional capital. I called my sister in Bafoussam, the west region's capital, and I asked her to go and look for my name on the list of recruits at the department of defense headquarters. She went and looked for my name, but it was not there.

What was I thinking, after all the signs of foul play? I called the captain to let him know my name was not on the list, and he acted like he was very surprised. But he had known it was impossible to just add my name to the list without going through a proper recruitment process.

I said, "Lord, I knew all along. I was insane to see all the red flags and continue anyway."

There was nothing I could do, and I did not have any means to go against the captain to try to recoup my money. I just said, "Lord, vengeance belongs to You, and You alone."

I always solicited God's help at the end of my failure when I hit a block, not at the beginning to know His prospect and will, because I was afraid of what He was going to say. I went first, and I put God behind, but He was still watching over me.

One thing I did not know was that He was working behind the scenes to make my dream come true. He knew I loved the military, and He took it at heart, or my prospect to join the military was already in His plan for my life.

He would, later on, prove to the captain he was wrong to abuse God's child, just like Joseph's brothers were proven wrong to mess with Joseph.

CHAPTER 10

My Dream

My life completely changed when I gave it to the Lord. My aspirations and my dream to have a better life became real through faith.

Also, as a firstborn child, I wanted to help my family by joining the military. Joining the Cameroonian military did not work, and I realized it was difficult to make a life in Cameroon due to the corrupt system of employment, which was dominated by relationship and not merit. I decided to try my best to leave Cameroon for Europe, in search of a better life, like all my friends, since my future was uncertain in Cameroon.

Some of my friends chose to immigrate to Europe by crossing the desert and the sea, and many died in the process by either drowning or dehydration. I chose to look for a job and make some money to finance my immigration or to use other legal means to obtain a visa and immigrate to Europe. So I sought help from relatives. I knew a miracle had to happen for me to leave the country.

I had an uncle who had lived in France for more than forty years, so I turned my attention to him. I let him know my intentions, and I requested his help. Once again, I put my trust in a man.

I was quickly deceived by my uncle, just like I had been deceived by the captain and others. He was not even willing to try because of previous failed experiences. At least he told me that even though he had the means to help me immigrate to Europe, it was very complicated. For the forty years he had spent in France, he had not been able to help anyone immigrate there.

I turned my attention to Ebenezer, my cousin in Spain. He and I grew up together, and we were very close. We shared the same dream. We went to different colleges, and our wishes were to be able to be successful in life and help our families. He had used an unconventional way to immigrate to Spain.

Since my uncle was not able to help me, I laid my problem at Ebenezer's feet, and he was willing to help me by using this unconventional way to immigrate to Europe because I desperately wanted to leave Cameroon. I was getting close to thirty without any future in sight. All I could see was my limitation, not my ability to do everything through the One that sustains me.

Ebenezer put me in contact with someone named Freeman, who had helped him immigrate to Spain. We met, and the plan was to use the same strategy he used to help my cousin. Freeman had a big brother in Spain, and he was a well-established businessman. He ran an organization placing soccer players on teams in Spain.

In Cameroon, Freeman was in charge of selecting and providing his brother with players. The organization was fake—it was just a way to help people immigrate to Spain. It worked for my cousin, and I was hoping it would work for me as well. So I went ahead, and I provided Freeman with all the required paperwork to prove I was a soccer player. I actually was a real soccer player.

The paperwork was to be sent to Freeman's brother in Spain so he could obtain admission to any soccer team, and the admission paper would serve me to apply for a visa. The whole process cost me 400,000.00 FCFA, which is less than a thousand dollars. So Freeman sent all my paperwork to his brother, and all we had to do was wait for the admission letter.

I visited Freeman more than ten times to follow up, and all he told me during my visits was to wait. I waited for months, but the letter never came. After months of waiting, I concluded that this was not going to work, and the only thing left to do was to get my 400,000.00 FCFA back.

I went to visit Freeman to let him know I wanted my money back because everything was conditioned on my traveling to Spain, but he was nowhere to be found. He had just vanished into the wilderness. Getting my money back became a problem, so I sought help. The Lord was there waiting for me to come to Him after my failure.

I could sense the Lord telling me, "Son, I am waiting for the day you start with Me."

I contacted one of my brothers in Christ named James. He was a police officer, and he had a lot of experience in catching bad guys. I did not know where Freeman lived because we always met at his parents' house. I explained the situation to James and gave him Freeman's description, then showed him Freeman's parents' house, where he hung out.

James came up with a game plan to get him. His plan was to post at least two officers on watch in front of Freeman's parents' house. As soon as they put eyes on him, they would follow him to his house.

He would soon fall into the trap.

One day, a police officer saw him at his parents' and followed him to his house. It was easy to get Freeman once his house was located. James and two of his officers went to Freeman's house at around 3 a.m., got him, and threw him in jail. That's how justice works in Cameroon.

I received the news from James that Freeman had been captured and was in jail. I got there as soon as I could to let Freeman know all I wanted was my money since he was not able to help me travel to Spain. I got my money back within twenty-four hours, and he was released from jail. We went our separate ways.

After another setback, I kept hoping and believing a miracle would eventually happen. It would happen, but not the way I had envisioned.

One day, I went to visit Ebenezer's mom to see how she was doing. She lived about a one-hour walk from our home. During my visit, I met one of Ebenezer's friends. He was a musician, but he was not popular. As we were chatting and sharing our miseries, he told a plan he had to immigrate to Spain by using his musician title to obtain a visa. He explained to me how he was going to create a group of musicians. The band had to include two guitarists, one drummer, one singer, and three backup singers.

He asked me if I was interested, and I said yes. I was going to be the drummer even though I had never played the drum in my entire life. This was true for everyone in the group, except for Ebenezer's friend, who was a true musician.

I said to myself, "The third time might be the charm." I had been praying all this time, but everything was overshadowed by my obsession with having a job and leaving the country.

The fake group, made up of desperate Cameroonians trying to leave the country, was formed in a blink of an eye. We met to discuss our strategy going forward and planned to obtain visas as musicians to go to Spain for a concert. But we needed an invitation coming from Spain to prove our legitimacy and our seriousness.

I used the payphone to call Ebenezer, who was very supportive of me and explained our situation and what we needed. He took the matter into his own hands as he had the first time and was able to find someone who owned a nightclub. He was successful in obtaining an invitation that would, later on, be sent and delivered to us by DHL.

After we gathered all our fake paperwork to submit for a visa application, we scheduled a date to travel to Yaoundé, where Spain's embassy was located. We took a bus as a group early in the morning to Yaoundé. After we arrived, we took a cab to the family home of one of our group members, where we would stay during the process.

We went to the embassy the next day and submitted our application for visas.

During the interview process, we explained to the consular that we were a group of musicians going to Spain for a concert, and our group invitation was included in our application. Our application was received, and we were asked to come back after two weeks for our application's result. We believed we had played our cards very well, and we had a good chance to obtain a visa. Actually, this was the first time I was so close to getting a visa.

So we all returned to our residence, and the waiting game began.

After two weeks, we went back and were told to come back after another two weeks because the result was not ready yet.

Because we had planned to spend a maximum of three weeks in Yaoundé, our subsistence money ran out, but we had no choice but to wait.

We went back after the extra two weeks were over for an update, and we were told the visa was denied.

One thing we did not know was the embassies in Cameroon and in all African countries had informants, and an investigating department was used for all types of visa application fraud. They actually found out we were not a legitimate group. People went to jail for the same situation.

I was very scared after this last attempt.

Most people, after many setbacks, turned to immigration through the desert and the Mediterranean Sea. More than eighteen thousand people have lost their lives in Mediterranean crossings since 2014, according to figures from both the UNHCR and the website of the UN's International Organization for Migration (IOM).

Since then, I really understood that immigrating was not an easy thing to do or go through. The Lord had many ways to make me understand He was the only One I could trust. I turned to the Lord Jesus for help again. He was always there waiting for me to return to Him, so I learned not to lean on my own understanding anymore but on the Lord. I strongly believed the Lord had a plan for me, and I put all my failures behind me, and I decided not to try or use any deceitful way to immigrate. If it was God's plan for me to leave the country, He would do so when the time was appropriate.

My faith faded because I was consumed with leaving the country. Also, I was just going from compromise to compromise. So instead of trying to make it happen by my own strength, I chose to do my part, which was to love Him with all my heart, and walk according to His word and put my trust in Him.

In the past, French and Spanish-speaking people in Africa wished to immigrate to Europe because of the language. It was more comfortable and easier to adapt to the European culture. I never considered immigrating to the United States of America because of the language barrier, and I believed at the time the United States was out of my league because I could not speak English. I was aware of people who had a lot of money but still could not immigrate to the US because obtaining a visa was tough.

I had forgotten that anything was possible with the Lord Jesus, and I did not know the Lord was working behind the scenes to open a door for a job.

Even today, things have not changed much in Cameroon. People are always looking for an opportunity to leave the country.

It took thirteen years after Joseph was thrown into the pit for him to see his dream come true. Just like Joseph, I was going to wait for the Lord.

According to Isaiah 40:31 (NIV), "But those who hope in the Lord will renew their strength. They will soar on wings like eagles; they will run and not grow weary; they will walk and not be faint."

CHAPTER 11

Running Like Joseph

I remember Joseph's story where he resisted committing adultery. Much like Joseph, I went through a similar story with my first daughter's mom, Jenette. This happened when my first love for Christ was still strong, and I was deeply anchored in Him. I regret saying this, but I still have never loved the Lord as I first loved Him at the beginning of my faith.

In our culture, back in Cameroon, everybody showed up at a funeral because it was always translated into a feast where people came to eat and drink. So when my dad passed away and we organized his funeral, both invited and uninvited people showed up, including Jenette. Jenette lived 150 miles away from our house, so she had to bring some clothes if she was going to spend the night, which she did.

The ceremony took place on a Saturday evening through Sunday morning, and most family members coming from a long distance were supposed to spend the night in our family's house and leave Sunday afternoon or Monday morning. But to my surprise, Jenette wanted to spend the night as well.

This would have been okay if she had wanted to spend the night at her sister's house, but she wanted to stay at my apartment and in my bed with me.

This was not okay.

At that period of my walk with Jesus, any type of compromise was like committing a crime because I would lose my joy and peace.

When it came time to go to bed, I found that she had brought all her belongings from my family house to my apartment and changed into a nightgown and lay on my bed. For me, there was nothing I could say or do except to run like Joseph.

I ran to my brother in Christ Nya, who lived a mile from our house—the same Nya I went to visit at the hotel LaFalaise, Akwa—and I explained the situation to him. He was gracious enough to let me spend the night at his place.

From my experiences with the Lord, I can sense when He is about to bless me. Most of the time, my blessings follow resistance to temptation or victory over sin—this formula is for the Lord and me only. The enemy comes between me and my blessings. He does everything to discourage me, and he tries to make me give up when the Lord is about to bless me. But God's grace will sustain me and power me to stand firm when I let Him be in control. The enemy will flee from me.

For me, there is always a price when I win over the enemy, which can manifest physically or spiritually. Spiritual manifestation comes by bringing a joy that transcends through my soul, and only Jesus and I can understand. Joy is just a part of His blessings because He also has a blessings jar in heaven, and He will physically bless me at the appointed time.

After a night with Nya, he and I returned to my mother's house to gauge the house's atmosphere. Guess what? There was chaos and agitation everywhere, orchestrated by Jenette.

I ran and asked Nya to follow because I knew there was nothing I could say or do to calm things down. I spent a week with Nya until everybody was gone before I went back home. I could then reason with my mom and put things back where there were before Jenette's visit. My mom loved Jenette for the simple reason that we had a child together, but she did not have a fear of God.

In Cameroon's culture, families encourage any relationship that results in the birth of a child to get married for the sake of the child. In my case, Jenette and

I had two different beliefs. I was a child of God, and she was not. The Bible says in 2 Corinthians 6:14 (NIV), "Do not be yoked together with unbelievers. For what do righteousness and wickedness have in common? Or what fellowship can light have with darkness?"

According to a source, Jenette told my mom that I did not spend the night with her in my apartment for no apparent reason. At least she was honest, not like Potiphar's wife, who did something and said the opposite to get out of trouble.

Jenette believed that my belief was a sect. The word "sect" did not sit well with our parents because belonging to the sect in Cameroon was the same as being a criminal. Jenette was acting desperate and crying when she told my mom what had happened. My mom, not knowing better, started to cry as well. She followed Jenette in her acting, and other people who sympathized with my mom followed her. It was chaos. People were crying everywhere because of Jenette's false story.

My mom believed Jenette, even though I never belonged to a sect. I was just a child of God and a firm believer. My mom had witnessed my transformative life through the Lord Jesus, so why was it that she believed Jenette?

It was because of the marabout. Jenette also told my mom that she knew this would happen because she had consulted a marabout to find out if she still had a chance to be with me. He told her there was a great chance for us to get back together, so rejection was a shock to her. My mom, being a fan of marabouts, believed her.

Jenette and I had spoken once or twice after I gave my life to Jesus, but she did not know to what extend I was serious in glorifying the name of the Lord in my life. I remember on one occasion I was talking to her about the Lord Jesus, and she mentioned that she met Christians in nightclubs all the time, but she did not believe that there were serious children of God who saw "visiting night" as a sin.

Look at Job's story and Joseph in the Bible. There, all resisted the enemy, and the Lord rewarded them. Remember to resist because even with the Lord, nothing comes without a fight. Joseph resisted Potiphar's wife, and he got promoted to prime minister; Job refused to curse God, and everything he lost was restored to him.

After I resisted Jenette, I got blessed with the job with which God's plan was associated. I do not have any answer as to what would have happened if I had not resisted the enemy.

From Apostle Paul, I learned to be content, resilient, and lean on God's grace. But from Joseph, I learned how to run. This skill has helped me over the years to get out of danger and physically and spiritually run toward safety in the Lord.

CHAPTER 12

Temporary and First Real Job

After years of searching, since I graduated from my vocation school in 1994, I landed a job in 2000. The job was temporary, and it was with a sub-contractor who had a contract with a prime contractor, the Cameroon Oil Transportation Company SA (COTCO), to provide food service during the construction of the pipeline.

Our team's job was to stay in the camp and prepare breakfast, a packed lounge, and dinner for prime contractor's employees working on the pipeline project, which was around ten miles away from the camp. Those employees included land surveyors, welders, electricians, and many more trades.

I got the job because of my name. One of the directors of the company was named Nana, and I presented myself to one of the recruiters as his family member. I was, but we were not close at all. I could not even meet him, but it worked; I got hired.

My job was to wash dishes, and I did it well, and I was loved by my boss, a French expat named Andrew. (I was so good at washing the dishes that when I moved to the US and worked for McDonald's, they wanted to keep me and make me a manager, but I had other aspirations. I got two jobs when I was living in Maryland because I needed money to pay back all the loans I had gotten to finance my trip to the US.)

The job lasted just six months, but since I proved myself to be a good employee, Andrew maintained me on the team for the next project. I was hired to serve food on a ship at the Douala shipyard.

Unfortunately, the job did not last either, and I was back to square one.

After years of praying and searching for a job, the Lord opened a door for an opportunity at a French highway construction company called SATOM. It was a miracle getting my first real job because getting a job in Cameroon was very difficult due to the corrupt system. But nothing was impossible for the Lord Jesus. The Lord used a brother in Christ to introduce me to the senior project manager of the company.

I had set aside a special day—Wednesday of every week—as a routine day to fast and pray for my job situation. On one of these special Wednesdays, I was fast-ing and pleading for God's intervention in my life. At around 11 a.m., I heard someone knock at my door. I opened the door, and there was my brother in Christ, Charly.

Charly and I went to the same church, and we were very close as brothers in the Lord. He and I had both been looking for a job, and he had been blessed to find one in the subject company months before me. I was surprised to see him because he did not visit me at home often. He was married, and I was always the one visiting him at his house.

I asked him, "What is the special occasion?"

Charly responded, "A senior project executive asked me if I knew a professional electrician who could run one of the bases during the highway construction project in Bertoua- Garoua-Mboulaï. I told him I had a good friend who would be a great fit for the job."

He asked me to dress up, and I did. I grabbed all my diplomas and certifications, and Charly and I went back to his workplace. He brought me to the French senior project executive's office and introduced me. He asked me to provide him with documents to qualify me for the job, and I provided him with all my credentials.

The senior project executive went through all my qualification documents and decided to put me through some testing to see if my technical knowledge of the electrical industry corresponded to the paperwork I had provided.

I was hired after a couple of months of testing, and the last step was to go to the jobsite so I could run a base. After everything was said and done, I traveled from Douala to Garoua-Mboulaï with a lot of new hires to the jobsite.

Charly had already made a name for himself in the few months he had worked there. He was known to be a good and trustworthy man because his conduct and love for Christ were some of the reasons the senior project executive had approached him to solicit his help. He chose him out of the at least three hundred employees at the base.

The trip was long, so we had to stop at the first base in Bertoua to eat and get some refreshments. After a brief break, we continued our trip to Garoua-Mboulaï to the second base, where I would take command of the electric department.

We finally got to the base, and I introduced myself to the personnel already on-site. The highway was at least 284 km long, and there were two bases: one was close to Bertoua city, and another one was close to Garoua-Mboulaï city. Garoua-Mboulaï city is in east Cameroon, where the country shares a border with the central Republic. The project's goal was to join the two countries with a highway.

The main function of each base was to provide logistics to expats (foreign workers), aggregate, and asphalt for the highway construction. My main function was to run a team of electricians to do all housing, generator, and audio-visual equipment installation and maintenance. The base housing was going to be just for expats. And the rest of the employees had to live outside of the base.

It did not take me long to find an apartment in the village. As soon as I found one, I settled down and bought all the necessary household materials like oil, a cooker, a bed, a pillow, utensils for the kitchen, bathing materials, etc. They gave me a week to settle down before I started the job.

God's plan for Joseph's life was already set in motion before he was born, but he started to gain much attention when he told his brothers he had dreamed that he was going to be their leader.

Much like with Joseph, God's plan in my life was already set in motion before I was born, and it started to unfold when I got a job, and I told folks in the electrical department that I was going to be their leader. It seemed to me that God paid particular attention to those who were hated because of His choosing.

CHAPTER 13

Much Like Joseph

As soon as my settling-in week was over, I went to work. I met some resistance from a co-worker named Judah as soon as I got there, and in the long run, with another co-worker named Bertrand.

Judah and Bertrand were like Joseph's brothers. The Lord used them to throw me into the pit like Joseph (my firing was my pit). There were three hired electricians already on the jobsite, and Judah was one of the hirings by Bertrand, a French foreign worker. The two others were named Francois and Luke. These electricians had worked for the company in the past; therefore, they knew that the best way to get hired was to show up at the jobsite to get recruited instead of applying at the main office in Douala.

Hiring in Douala was political and corrupt and mostly for high-ranking personnel. But I was an exception because I was one of the blessed ones who got hired at the main office in Douala. It was God's plan for my life. I was hired to be their boss, and I was also the youngest person and the most educated. Judah and Bertrand did not like me because I disturbed an order already established in the electrical department.

The base had a director who administrated the project and a senior executive director who ran the technical department. He was my first boss, and his name was Mr. Giraud. He was actually the director who hired me, and he was the head of all technical departments, which included electrical, plumbing, mechanical, and building construction.

Each of those leadership positions was held by a French foreigner. I was hired to be number two in the electrical leadership department, but I had no idea of the spiritual fight I was getting myself into. They would try to physically win the battle, which was already won spiritually because I was predestined for that job.

The first phase of the job was to work with all other departments to build permanent housing for expats. My job as second in command after Bertrand was to coordinate all electrical installation and maintenance. It took my team and me at least a year to build the entire base. After all the construction was completed, all we had to do was maintenance. My leadership was confirmed by the grace of God through my expertise and knowledge in the field. I was able to resolve issues my colleagues could not.

News traveled fast that I was the best electrician who could solve any electrical issue. The water plant for the base was one of the projects that made me very famous. I conceived and executed an auto system that would work to feed the entire base with portable water. In the process, I won the hearts and support of two of my co-workers, but Judah did not take it very well. He started to plot against me, just like Joseph's brothers.

Just like Joseph's brothers hated him so much that they wanted him dead, so did Judah. He wanted me out of the job or the picture as quickly as possible because I was always called to fix things. Judah and Bertrand believed their jobs were at risk.

Both men, especially Judah, started to undermine my leadership by purposely damaging electrical equipment to make me look bad. They spread false rumors about my competence when things were going wrong. Judah and Bertrand became even more jealous because I was able to fix any malicious electrical problem created by Judah. Bertrand knew what was going on, but he did not say or do anything to prevent Judah from doing it.

At that point, they were convinced that I was an enemy. They wanted to get rid of me because their jealousy grew to hatred, just like Joseph's brothers, and they started to formulate their plan to get me fired. They believed that their jobs were on the line because I was the man to go to for any electrical issue.

My routine on the job was to make my rounds every morning to make sure the electrical equipment, such as generators, panel boards, lighting, etc., worked properly. I could tell when an electrical issue had been caused by sabotage.

But the Lord gave me the wisdom to continue to extend His love to both Judah and Bertrand and to behave such that the Lord would not find any wrongdoing in my attitude and behavior by loving them.

Judah built a strong relationship with Bertrand, and they plotted to have me fired or worse. But Mr. Giraud—my first boss and the head of all technical departments—was not aware of my situation. He would, later on, be transferred to a different country, and I would not have any support except the Lord Jesus.

I did a little investigation after I got to Garoua-Mboulaï. I found there was not an active biblical church to go to for worship on Sundays. I took the initiative to find some children of God on the jobsite so we could start a church or a prayer group. I was three years old in the faith, and my love for the Lord was so strong, I wanted to keep the flame going. Nothing, not even a city without a church, would have stopped me. God blessed my effort, and I was able to find some brothers with whom I could start a prayer group.

We prayed two times a week. Each of us had his own challenge at work and in his personal life. One thing I learned from the prayer team was that everyone on the jobsite knew there were some rivalries going on between electricians in the electrical department, and it was always a subject of our prayer. God preserved and protected me against any plan of the enemy. We were a very dynamic, faithful, and strong group, and we constantly prayed for our spiritual growth, love for others, and forgiveness for those who persecuted us.

We were also able to bring the love of Jesus to others on the jobsite. The construction project was to last at least four years, and we were determined to see it to the end by God's grace. Even though my leadership was strongly contested, the Lord gave me the grace to continue to lead and to do my job.

When the active highway construction project was close to completion and there was not another project scheduled to transfer employees to, the company laid people off. This practice was normal, but in most cases, essential employees were saved.

My case was different. Even though I was an essential employee, I was still one of the first people on the chopping block. Since Judah did not like me, he was successful in convincing Mr. Bertrand to have me fired.

I had a higher pay grade and was too expensive to the company, according to him. Bertrand bought into that distorted assumption. He did not just buy into Judah's assumption—he also cosigned for it.

Bertrand and Judah were about the same age, and they shared a lot of things in common; they were both womanizers, they were not Christ-followers, and many other things. Bertrand was the only one close to the project director—who was a French expat like him—to report anything from the electrical department. He used the opportunity to talk to the director about letting me go since everything was under control and all they had to do was equipment maintenance.

Bertrand and Judah's wishes were granted, and I was one of the first employees to be fired from the project. I felt like I had been thrown into the pit, which would be very difficult to get out of.

After I got fired, I thanked the Lord for the opportunity to serve on the project and for the difference I made in people's lives by preaching the gospel. I took my time to say goodbye to everyone on the jobsite. A lot of co-workers were upset to find out I was leaving, and some even predicted I would be coming back because I was the only electrician who knew how to work on all media equipment and all electrical systems.

But I did not know that the Lord was speaking through my co-workers.

This was how the firing was supposed to go down: The base director would send a request to all department heads to require all the names of people who could be dismissed. In my case, the department head was Mr. Bertrand. Because I was number two in leadership of our department, Mr. Bertrand would then ask me for names of potential employees to let go. I would come up with that list and give it to Mr. Bertrand. He would pass it on to the director, who would finally make public the list of employees to let go.

I was known to be the number two on paper, but not in practice.

What happened was that Mr. Bertrand had conspired with his partner in crime and drinking buddy Judah behind my back. They came up with my name to be fired, and I was the first and the only one on the list among four electricians working in our team. So when I received my termination letter, I knew I was no longer part of the project. The only thing left for me to do was to pack all my stuff and head back home to Douala, where God's miracles would continue to take place in my life.

Before heading to Douala, I said goodbye again to my friends and my brothers in Christ. My firing raised a lot of questions among my friends because I was known to be the best at my job. Nevertheless, I took the trip back home. It was tough for me to believe what had just happened to me. I had put all my hope in that job because I believed the job could have helped me change my future by financing my travel abroad. I chose to stay positive and hope for the best.

But it was not easy. According to Philippians 4:6-7 (NIV), "Do not be anxious about anything, but in every situation, by prayer and petition, with thanksgiving, present your requests to God. And the peace of God, which transcends all understanding, will guard your hearts and your minds in Christ Jesus."

This scripture was hard to follow, especially when I believed I was a victim of an injustice. However, I had no choice but to trust the Word of Jesus. It was His will for me not to damage my health by dwelling on something I did not have any control over.

I believe that was Joseph's attitude as well when he was thrown into the pit, trusting the Lord. Joseph's brothers did not know they were instruments that the Lord was using to accomplish His plan in Joseph's life, to bring him from the pit to prime minister and to glory.

Bertrand and Judah did not know that they were instruments in God's hand to bring me from pit to glory.

CHAPTER 14

Playing the Green Card Lottery

After Joseph was thrown into the pit, one of his brothers pleaded for his life. As a result, Joseph was sold to some merchants passing by instead of being left to die in the pit.

There was a transaction between Joseph's brothers and the merchants, which resulted in Joseph's going to Egypt with the merchants. Douala was the place where my transaction took place, where I played the lottery.

I did not call my family to let them know I was on my way back home, and everyone was surprised to see me earlier than expected. I explained what had happened and the reason for my dismissal. My family was more concerned than me because I was the breadwinner of the entire family. We spent hours chatting, and we went to bed afterward.

One part of me was happy to be back home because I was leaving behind a lot of dramas. But the other part was not happy at all because I had a plan built upon that job, and everything was contingent open finishing the project, so I could make enough money for my dream of leaving the country to come true.

The money saved would have served as caution or proof of funds to apply for a college in Europe in the hope of being accepted. Once accepted, I would apply for a visa to leave Cameroon in search of a better life.

I felt like my dream had gotten shut down—crushed—because it had taken me years to get my first real job. I wondered how many more years it would take me to find another job to be able to see my dream to leave Cameroon come true. Probably like Joseph, I wondered how to get out of the pit.

A lot of questions went through my mind, and I did not have any correct answers. I lost hope. I also had some concerns about the people I had talked to about God's love on the jobsite; they might perceive God as weak, not being able to stand up for His children.

One thing I did not know was that God's plan was at work in my life; the promise the Lord made in the book of Jeremiah was in action. According to Jeremiah 29:11 (NIV), "'For I know the plans I have for you,' declares the Lord, 'plans to prosper you and not to harm you, plans to give you hope and a future.'"

It was very difficult to hold on to God's promise when I was going through this tribulation and challenge. I had experienced life challenges before, but I did my best to trust in the Lord. I tried to move on because I knew the Lord would never fail me.

After I got myself together, I was ready to start a new chapter of my life. The day after I got home, the pain of losing a strategy job was still there. I asked God why He had let this happen to me because, according to my understanding, it looked like this was a clear win for the enemy. But it was not true and steadfast. Even Joseph's brothers thought that they had clearly won their battle with Joseph.

The next morning, I decided it was time to let some of my church-member friends know I was back in town. The first one I went to visit at his workplace was Mr. Nya.

Mr. Nya was a personal taxi driver working for the hotel called LaFalaise, located in the urban area of Douala called Akwa. I did not see the brother in question when I got to the hotel because he was driving a customer around the town. I met another friend named Claude instead, who was there for the same objective— meeting brother Nya. He was surprised to see me because he did not know I was back in town already. So we chatted for a while, and I told him my story. Since we had both missed our friend Nya, we started heading home.

On our way home, brother Claude talked to me about the United States of America lottery program, which consisted of filling out a form and submitting it for entry for a selection for the DV-2002 program by mail to the state department in Kentucky. Today, everything is done electronically. It seemed like the lottery program had been going on for a while, but this was my first time hearing about it. He also told me the form had to be mailed outside of Cameroon because anything mailed from Cameroon would be destroyed by post office employees because they did not want anyone to be successful in winning the lottery. He added that brother Kesey from our church was the brother with more information about the program, and he could help me fill out the form.

Since I was interested in playing the lottery program, we headed directly to my brother Kesey to get more information and some help filling out the lottery form. Kesey was very happy to see me as well. He did not know I was back because I had been fired from my job, but he would find out later on. So we chatted about the US lottery program, and he confirmed that it was legitimate. He had helped a lot of people fill out the forms.

I know there are a lot of people in the US who do not know anything about this lottery program but rest assured, it does not involve money.

Kesey got me a form and confirmed that it had to be mailed outside of the country. Filling out the form was very simple. It just required your name, date of birth, place of birth, a four-by-four photo, your level of education, and your signature.

So I filled out the form, and the question of mailing it outside of the country arose and needed to be resolved. As I was trying to solve the mailing problem, brother Marcel came into my mind. Marcel's boss traveled to France to buy used auto parts to resell in Cameroon. So I contacted Marcel to see if it was possible for his boss to carry my letter to France and mail it off from there to the United States of America.

Marcel asked me, "What importance does the letter have to be posted in France?"

I explained to him about the lottery program, and I told him I had been advised not to mail it here because it would be destroyed or thrown in the trash.

After I explained this to Marcel, he became very interested in the program as well, so I asked him to come and join us at brother Kesey's house. He came and filled out two forms—one for himself and one for his fiancée. After we completed the forms, Marcel took our three envelopes to his boss, who was actually leaving for France in a couple of days. He was able to mail off those forms from France to the US as soon he got there. He called us from France to confirm the posting.

Everything just happened like it was predestined to happen. Jesus was behind it all, and He was connecting all the dots as He did for Joseph.

CHAPTER 15

Return to Work & God's Glorification

After I filled out the lottery paperwork and every-thing was mailed off, I was back praising the Lord and doing His will. I was a young leader in my church, and I was very active in evangelizing, preaching, and counseling new believers. There were about two hun-dred people in our church, and I knew each member's name, family, and house.

One day, I was going about my business, and I had a phone call from the project director in Bertoua. It was approximately three weeks after being fired from my job.

The director had noticed that nothing was working since I left, and he wanted me back as soon as possible to fix everything. I asked him what it meant that noth-ing was working, and he responded by saying the water plan, audio vision, TV, and many other things were no longer working properly. At that point, I knew I had the upper hand on him, and the Lord had given me a victory over my enemies. I knew I was in a strong position to negotiate a new contract term. I said to the director that my return was conditional, and he quickly asked me to list my wants.

I laid out all my conditions. For one, I requested to select my own team. Second, I asked that my salary be doubled. Third, I requested a personal car. And last, that I would be the only head of the electrical department, and he would be my boss, nobody else.

To my surprise, he said yes to all four conditions. Now it was for me to pack and go back to work. I was so happy because I was going back to make more money to follow my immigration dream, but I didn't even imagine the Lord had more in store for me, and this was just a step in the right direction.

I took a company car at the main office in Douala to travel to the base in Garoua-Mboulaï, and as soon I got back to work, I met the director. All my conditions were honored. My salary was doubled, Bertrand was fired, and Judah had disappeared from the jobsite before I even got there. The director provided me with a new personal truck for service, and I selected to work with the two remaining electrician friends I had left behind when I was fired.

I believed this was a miracle from God, and even my friends on the jobsite recognized the power of our God and that I served a living God. My faith was known by everyone, and that was one of the reasons why my direct leadership hated me so much. I had been going around during my spare time talking about the love of Jesus to people.

It took my two electrician friends, named Francois and Luke, and me a couple of weeks to have everything up and running again. Our prayer group was restored as well, and life was going perfectly. Once everything was repaired, all we had to do every day with my team was just routine maintenance of equipment.

After my return to the jobsite, the only news I had from Judah was that he was hospitalized for a medical condition no one knew about. I took it upon myself to pay him a visit at the hospital to wish him well and talk to him about Jesus' love.

When he saw me, he cried and begged for my for-giveness, which I granted. After we chatted, I told him about the Lord Jesus and forgiveness. I also prayed for him before I left the hospital.

The three weeks I spent in Douala, doing all my pa-perwork and making transactions with my brothers in Christ to play the lottery, was like the time Joseph's brothers were selling him to the merchant.

Later on, in Joseph's story, God would bring Joseph's brothers to Egypt to confuse them and glorify His name because they had messed with an apple of God's eye. Jesus planned my return to my job to confuse my enemies, who had taken a victory lap when I got fired because they had messed with an apple of God's eye as well.

In order to bring Joseph's brothers to Egypt to confuse them, the Lord had to create starvation in the entire region, and He did a similar thing for me. In order to confuse my enemies, the Lord had to mess up all the electrical systems so I could be called back to my job.

CHAPTER 16

Winning the Green Card Lottery

Four months into the job, I got a phone call from my uncle back in Douala. It was about a letter he had received from the provenance of the United States of America. I told him I did not have any family members living in the US, and I was not sure the letter was for me. He advised me to come and see the letter. So I explained the situation to my boss, and I asked him for a week off, which he granted me to go back to Douala to resolve whatever misunderstanding was going on.

After I arrived at Douala, I went straight to see my uncle at his workplace. I met him in his office, and he gave me the envelope. As soon as I opened it, I read, "Congratulations, you have won the United States lottery." I had completely forgotten about the lottery I had played about five months before and that I had used my uncle's office as a return address.

I was overcome with emotion. This meant I had been randomly selected to immigrate to the United States of America. If I met all the requirements, and if I passed the visa screening process, I would be heading to the US.

Millions of people around the world played this lottery every year, but very few were selected, and there was a limit on how many applicants could have been selected in each given year.

Many rich and poor people from underdeveloped African countries had embarked on the dangerous journey for Europe in hopes of a better life. So immigrating to the United States of America was a big deal because the US is blessed beyond measure. People were ready to spend millions to come to the US, but they could not because it was tough and complicated to obtain a visa. The US has tough immigration laws that do not give privilege to anybody, and everyone has to meet the immigration requirements to be able to obtain a visa.

The door that seemed to be closed to others was wide open for me because I serve a God of impossibilities. Tough immigration laws, in addition to the language barrier, were reasons why I had never thought about immigration to the United States.

I had no choice but to call my boss and explain my situation to him, and I recommended Francois to replace me on the job. He understood my situation. I submitted my resignation to take care of my visa application.

My English reading and comprehension were very poor. I could barely speak or write English, and I had to have a trusted English speaker to help with all processes. Thank God for Kesey, who helped me play, because I went to him for help. Kesey and I spent three to four months filling out the paperwork.

A high school certificate, medical exams, background check, and other documents were required for the visa application process. I also needed a sponsor in the US to provide me with an affidavit of support.

When everything was completed and my affidavit of support was in hand, I took a bus from Douala to Yaoundé, where the US embassy was located. I got off the bus and took a cab to the embassy. As soon as I got there, I was escorted inside by a security guard. It was a tough day. I was panicking. I was anxious and afraid of losing my only chance to immigrate and to leave the country. I prayed and asked God for His grace.

I provided all the required documents. While in the interview process, the lady conducting my interview noticed I could not speak English. She asked me how I would communicate once in the US. I replied that I was going to learn to write and speak English once I was in the US because I would have no choice.

Once she went through all my paperwork and found me eligible for a visa, she asked me to come back in a couple of weeks to pick up my package, which included my passport with a visa and envelope, which I was supposed to give to customs at the airport in the US.

After two weeks, I went to pick up my package, and the panic attack stopped. I was so happy. I had finally done it like it was through my effort. In that moment of happiness, I had a flashback of all the negative things that were said to me by different people, including my dad, such as, "You will never succeed in life; you are a lost cause; nothing good will come from you," and many other things.

However, the Lord reminded me He was the only one who held and decided for the future, and I should listen to Him instead of listening to mean people.

I went back to Douala with my passport and package in my hand, and I managed to come up with enough money to buy my plane ticket. I scheduled my departure date to the US.

Everything was done in secrecy because I did not want to lose my life by letting anybody around me know I was leaving the country. Some Cameroonians were very wicked, and they could have come after me if they found out I had obtained a visa to leave the country.

They could have tried to kill me by poisoning me or even attacking me physically at night to get my passport because they wanted me to be miserable and stay miserable like them.

All my bags were prepared in advance the night before my travel, so when I woke up the morning of my departure day, I was ready to go to the airport. I took a cab with my closest family members to the Douala International Airport. When we got there, I went through all the procedures, and I waited to board the plane to the US. I chatted with my family for a couple of hours. When it was time to leave, I embarked and took off for the US.

My mom was so happy because she had seen me struggle to leave the country and make a life of my own. The news got into the neighborhood that I had left for the US. Many people, including some of my closest friends, did not believe it.

For me, winning the lottery, as well as Joseph being sold to an Egyptian, were our passports to our promised and respective land.

CHAPTER 17

Selection's Process

I have explained a little bit about the process and what happened after my envelope was mailed off to the US. My lottery form got entered into a computerized system, and I was randomly selected.

The computerized system selects few applicants, and it was a miracle for me to be chosen. The lottery program was played by millions of people in every single country in the entire world, so this was really God in action in my life. A lot of people enter it year after year and are never successful, but by God's grace, I was successful on my first try.

The Department of State in Kentucky sent me a letter to notify me of my selection, which included a letter of congratulations; a list of forms to be filled out—such as a visa application; a list of medical exam tests to be done with the names of accredited doctors authorized to perform those exams; a list of documents to be provided—such as birth certificate, high school diploma, vaccination card; and affidavit of support to be completed by someone living in the US who would support me financially and provide me with a place to stay.

Without those documents, especially the high school diploma and affidavit of support, I could not have traveled to the US.

The affidavit of support coming from the US was one of the toughest documents to have because it was difficult to find someone willing to support me financially, give me a place to stay, and help me integrate into the new culture.

At the time, I did not know anybody in the US who could provide me such a document, but I was lucky to have a friend whose brother lived in the US. I turned to him for help.

I explained my situation to my friend Jonathan. He was gracious enough to contact his brother, Paul, in the US to help me with the affidavit of support. Finding someone who would take the risk to support me was not easy, but the Lord had everything planned out. God touched Paul's heart, and he was able to help me with an affidavit of support.

After I filled out and gathered all information, I just waited for the interview date since it was already scheduled by the State Department.

CHAPTER 18

Moving to the US

Joseph's final destination, according to the Lord's plan in his life, was Egypt, to become the leader he had dreamed of becoming.

My next destination was the US.

I landed at the Dulles Airport in Virginia, in the United States, for the first time in March 2002, according to the Lord's plan and grace. It is very important to know that coming to the US is not the main issue here in the book, but that the Lord always meticulously works behind the scenes, especially when we are wondering if He knows our name, our struggle, or if He even cares about us to accomplish whatever plan He has for our life. If we just submit to Him, by being obedient to His word, He will work our salvation so we can be like Him. The truth is, the Lord is always there working for our good and watching over us.

Do not get me wrong here because coming to the United States of America was a great exploit for me since it was always my dream to leave Cameroon in search of a better life in Europe. But the Lord decided otherwise and brought me here to the US. This was His plan for my life anyway, and I was and still am very grateful.

After I got off the airplane, I had to go through customs to present my passport with a visa stamp in it, and also to drop off the envelope package given to me when I received my visa at the customs office at the airport. When I finished with customs, I headed outside to wait for my ride.

We had landed late in the afternoon, and as night fell, I enjoyed the beauty of the city. I waited for Paul to come and pick me up at the airport, chatting with the Cameroonians I had traveled with.

After a while, the ride of one of the Cameroonians came to pick him up. We introduced ourselves to each other, and he happened to know Paul; I mentioned that Paul was supposed to come and pick me up from the airport. Seeing that he hadn't arrived, this man offered to give me a ride as well. I accepted and was even more amazed as we drove down a four-lane highway because I had never experienced anything like that city before.

We got to his house, and he called Paul to let him know I was there waiting for him. Paul came to get me. During our trip to his house, he apologized for forgetting to pick me up at the airport as he should have, and I said it was okay because we all forget sometimes. But God was good. He provided me with transportation from the airport by someone I did not even know.

We got to Paul's house, and I was happy to be there.

We chatted a little bit to get to know each other; I thanked him for his support, and he showed me my room. I went to bed, as it was very late at night. I was going to stay with him until I found a stable home. I had never met him before, and this was the first time we saw each other, so we chatted again in the morning, and he told me to feel free in his home, and he showed me the refrigerator and a little bit around the house, and he left for work.

I spent my first day in the United States wondering what I was going to do with my life. Everything I had seen so far was a sign that life here would be very different from life back home, and I knew I would be blessed.

When Paul came back from his job, he cooked, ate, and took a few minutes of break. After his break, he asked me to come and sit down so we could talk about some ground rules. He said I had two weeks to live with him, and after that, I had to find a new place to live because that was the length of time he had agreed upon with his brother, Jonathan.

I was very thankful for what Paul had done for me. He did not just provide me with a shelter; he also provided me with an affidavit of support for my visa application, without which I would not have been able to come to the US. It was a mandatory document that I needed to provide to guarantee I would not be a charge or a burden to the US government once I was here. People who provide the affidavit of support to lottery winners take a lot of responsibility because they become your legal guardian, and they become responsible for all your actions once in the country, and they have the obligation to ensure your integration.

After a week of living with Paul, I called friends and family members back home to find out who had a family member here in the US with whom I could live until I had all my papers. At the time, I did not know the timeframe it would take to receive my papers, but it would ultimately take me at least four months to receive my green card. After my green card, I had to go apply for my social security, which would take another two to four weeks. Until then, I could not do anything; I could not work or apply for any job. My situation was complicated.

But after many phone calls to Cameroon, I was lucky to find out I had a cousin living in Silver Spring, Maryland, named Jacqueline. I was given her contact number, and I called her to introduce myself for the first time. She recognized me and agreed to give me a place to stay.

After living with Paul for two weeks, I thanked him for everything he had done for me. He was gracious enough to give me a ride to Jacqueline's house in Maryland. I acclimated myself at Jacqueline's house and could sense a brighter future. In the meantime, I waited for my green and social security cards so I could start looking for a job.

Jacqueline was a single parent. The atmosphere in my new house was fine. We talked regularly, and I let her know my intention to go back to school and finish my electrical engineer degree. I spent my time watching TV and reading the newspaper as a hobby to learn English.

One day, I came across an article titled "Joining the US Military" about how the military would be a good place to make a career. It got my attention since I loved the military. However, since I was limited in what I could do because of my English, I did not have my SSC and my green yet, and I thought I would not meet the age requirement because I was thirty-two years old at the time, I gave up any consideration of joining the military. I forgot all about it.

After a few weeks of living with my cousin, she wanted to set up some ground rules like Paul. During our conversation, she gave me four months to live with her, and after four months, I would have to look for my own place. When our conversation was over, I asked myself what was going on or what was wrong with me such that people, including my blood relatives, were just giving me a short period of time to live with them. I was confused because she was my cousin, and family takes care of family no matter what, because that was/is how it worked back home.

In Cameroon, a family member could just move in and stay with you forever in your house because it was part of the culture to take care of a family member. This was a culture shock for me because this would be the second time I was put out of the house for no apparent reason.

I had already visited the college to have information on the electrical engineer program before Jacqueline told me how long I was going to stay with her, and I wondered what would become of my dream to go to school. I thought this was an American culture thing—kicking friends or a family member out of the house, especially when they do not have anywhere to go—but it was not.

I was lucky to receive my green card and then my social security card four months after entering the US. I went out as soon as I received those cards to find a job. I walked miles every day looking for a job because I did not have a driver's license. I went everywhere by foot, and I was not a stranger to the practice because it was by foot that I went to school and by foot that I had looked for a job in Cameroon.

One day during my walk, I located an Indian church under construction, and I went to the construction site to ask for a job. I was blessed that the electrical engineer for the project was on the jobsite, and I asked to talk to him. I used the little English I had learned so far by watching TV and reading the newspaper to introduce myself, and I told him about my electrical background in Cameroon.

He believed and trusted me, and he gave me a job as an electrician helper. His company had jobs in Maryland and in Virginia, and I learned to use the metro to go from job to job. I was always picked up by one of the electricians or the boss himself at the train station terminal and taken to the jobsite. I was amazed at how easy it was to find my first job in the US.

Before my four months were over, I found a room in somebody's house, and I moved out of Jacqueline's house. I was on my own.

CHAPTER 19

Struggling for a Home Church

I was working on integrating into the US culture. I established a routine of things I used to do back home in my life, such as going to church, daily Bible study and prayer, etc. But early in my church search, I could not find a church in the US that suited or met my spiritual demands. I did not connect with any that I visited.

The doctrine was all about prosperity, which was not the essence of my faith, and no emphasis was put on the fear or the holiness of God. Matthew 6:33 (NIV) says to "seek first his kingdom and his righteousness, and all these things will be given to you as well." Health and wealth are gifts from God to humankind, but love and righteousness are what God commends.

I had just left a church in Cameroon where members were bonded as a family. It was difficult to adjust to any other church unless I could find something similar.

My parents were not educated, and in our culture in Cameroon, parents in general never showed love or said "I love you" to their children. My dad and mom were no different. So there was a great need for love in my life because I did not receive any love as a child, and it created a vacuum. All I had was the love given to me by the church, which filled up that vacuum by accepting me, treating me with respect, protecting me, and above all, loving me without condition. A love that empowers to love everyone, to dream anything, and to trust and believe in anything.

I looked for that kind of church when I got to the US. I was again thirsty and longing for a church where love was the center of everything, a church where everybody was welcomed and shown love, and a church that feared the Lord.

Back in Cameroon, we were a community of believers and fellowshippers. We tended to pray a lot, attend religious services regularly, and evangelize more, and we gave a considerable and important place to our Lord in our hearts.

According to a recent Pew Research Center study, "At the same time, Christians in the United States also have comparatively high levels of commitment to their faith."

I knew there was a church for me. So I kept looking for years to try to find something close to what I had back home. I tried to be content with a couple of churches that I found, but it was not easy.

While I struggled to find a home church, I got some more information about my eligibility to join the US military. I had two objectives, one was to find a church, and the other one was to join the US military.

CHAPTER 20

Determination to Join the US Military

I had not been successful in joining Cameroon's military, but God had another plan for me. By His grace, I was given an opportunity to join the US military.

While I worked as an electrician helper during the day, I took English classes in different high schools at night. One day, as I was going to work, I saw a big military recruiting sign at Prince George's Plaza metro station area in Hyattsville, Maryland, and I remembered seeing the same ad in the newspaper.

I went to the recruitment station to get some information about the recruitment process, especially to find out about the age limit because I was thirty-two at the time. To my surprise, they told me I was still eligible because the age limit was thirty-four. I was also told I had to pass the ASVAB test to join the military. They told me where to find the ASVAB textbook for test preparation. But they did not believe I could pass the test because my English was very poor, and I had a hard time communicating with them.

Joining the military was what I had always wanted, so I went home and searched for an English as a Second Language School. I found a lot of high schools with ESL training programs. I chose one in Hyattsville, in downtown Maryland, close to Prince George Metro station, to take some courses to better my English comprehension and speaking.

I bought the ASVAB study test book, and I took ESL after working hours. So I was taking classes and studying English and using my textbook to practice at the same time. After three months of study, I decided to take my first test, and my result was miserable. I failed with flying colors, but it did not stop me from continuing to learn.

Failure is certain when you give up trying. I was resolute to cut back my working hours to concentrate on studying and passing the ASVAB test because my age was against me. I was getting close to thirty-three, and thirty-four was around the corner.

After three to four months of intense study, I went back for the second time to take the test, and guess what? I failed again. I was told that if I failed the third time, I would have to wait six months before I could take any test, and it did not sound good to me.

I didn't really have any friends in Maryland, so I decided to quit my job and move to Georgia to live with my friend and brother in Christ, Marcel. I forgot to mention that Marcel's wife (at the time his fiancée) had won the lottery, and Marcel won as well by association. The prophecy spoken to us became a reality because the Lord is faithful.

We had both won the lottery, and we had gone to different destinations in the United States of America. I had flown to Maryland while Marcel and his wife had flown to Georgia. My other friend, Jean, had gone to France.

I packed all my belongings and took the Greyhound bus to Georgia. I traveled for hours, and Marcel picked me up at the bus station. The next morning, we spoke about our past and how the Lord had blessed us beyond measure.

I spoke to him about my dream of joining the US military and the process I had started in Maryland. I went to work by using a computer to look for English as a Second Language schools around me, and I was able to find a school where I signed up for classes to continue learning.

I also decided to take a boot camp approach because there was no room for another mistake. So I decided to study all day and all night for the test. I concentrated and studied and was scheduled to take the third test exam by the end of five months.

After my boot camp was over, I went to Georgia's processing center to take my third exam test. I passed the test this time with flying colors. Everyone at the processing center was surprised because I did way better on my third exam than I had done on my two previous attempts.

They were so surprised that they could not believe it was me who took the test. So they asked me to take another test. I took the test for the fourth time with someone observing me. I aced it again, and they had no choice but to accept the result.

The Navy used the same software in all fifty states, and it was easy to see my previous score and the comments entered by my previous recruiter in Maryland. It was true that my comprehension and my English reading were getting better, but my knowledge in math, science, and physics also helped me a lot on the test.

After I passed the physical and Armed Services Vocational Aptitude Battery standards test, I was then told to choose a branch of service. I chose the Navy. The Navy needed personnel at the time because it was just after 9/11, and the US was getting ready to start another war with Afghanistan.

A service liaison counselor told me about jobs opportunities available in the Navy. He explained each program and answered any questions I had. My first choice was the Seabees, a construction battalion. But I was not a US citizen, which was one of the requirements. I went for IT, but IT had the same requirement. I had no choice but to take what was offered to me: a fireman job.

CHAPTER 21

Joining the Military & Marijuana Problem

To join the military, I had to go through a medical examination at the MEPS (Military Entrance Processing Stations). MEPS determines the applicant's physical qualifications, aptitude, and assessed moral standards for all recruited personnel in all branches of military service.

According to GoArmy.com:

> The physical examination consists of height and weight measurements, hearing and vision examinations, drug and alcohol tests,

urine and blood tests, muscle group and joint maneuvers—in underclothing—complete physical examination and interview, specialized test, and a questionnaire for medical history.

I believe you are asking yourself how I went through all these processes without knowing English. At this point, I could read, and I could speak a little bit, but listening was still a problem because people spoke so fast.

I successfully went through each of those steps of the medical examination, but there was one problem. During the exam, the MEPS doctor asked me a series of questions, and there was one particular question that I was not sure about the answer I gave.

The doctor asked me, "Have you ever smoked or taken marijuana, and if yes, how many times?"

I misunderstood the question. I thought the doctor was asking if I was married because I heard the sound of "marriage" in "marijuana."

Because I had been married once, my response to the doctor was, "Yes."

Thank God, after everything was said and done, we all sat down to review our record, and this particular question was on my mind since I was so unsure about the answer I had given to the doctor.

I asked one of my friends, who was also a recruit, to help me review my medical record to find out the answer to my question. I explained to him that I was not sure about a particular question. He agreed to help, so we went through my medical record, and surely, I gave a wrong answer to the marijuana question.

According to my answer, I had smoked marijuana once in my life. So I went back to see the doctor and explained to him that my answer to the marijuana question was wrong because I never took marijuana, and I did not even know what it looked like. I could see the doctor laughing and, after having fun, he corrected my medical record. This mistake could have caused me not to join the military, but the Lord intervened through a friend and saved me from embarrassment.

I completed the examination process and moved to the next step, which was to go through a final interview and fingerprinting check. I then received a pre-enlistment briefing and took the oath of enlistment.

Our departure date was scheduled for November 2, 2002. After we finished with the examination, they had us spend two days at a hotel, where we were picked up by bus to Hartsfield-Jackson Atlanta International Airport. From there, we all flew to O'Hare International Airport in Chicago, Illinois.

There were at least three buses waiting for us at O'Hare for the long trip to Great Lakes. I was used to the warm weather in Cameroon, so the weather in Maryland and Georgia was a shock for me. When I stepped off the bus in Great Lakes, there was ice and snow everywhere, and it was freezing. I wondered if I was going to survive the weather and finish the month and a half of training I was supposed to do in the Great Lakes.

We all got off the bus and went to the welcome center. We were shaved, then took a shower and went to bed. We woke up refreshed the next morning. We got our uniforms and shoes and discovered that our plan for the day was already established. The recruit training command's plan was to assign each of us to a division where we would be trained for the next month and a half. Each group had leadership already assigned to them.

The leadership was composed of three recruit division commanders. Division commanders (RDCs) were chief petty officers, and their job was to mold us into sailors. In my division, one of the RDCs noticed early on that I had an English comprehension issue because when he asked me to do something, I would do the opposite.

He called me to his office to discuss the issue. He told me that he would take me out of the current division to a different division where I would learn English. So I was moved to the new division, and all I did was learn English.

For four months, I learned how to read and write English. After the four months of intensive English learning were completed, I successfully graduated from my English learning program. I packed my belongings and moved to another new division that had been assigned to me, this time to graduate boot camp.

All we learned in the new division was purposely set to impart us with Navy values, commitment, and courage within a team environment. I started the process all over again. I spent our first week going through medical, administration, and dental screening. The following two weeks were very difficult because I had to adjust my mind and body to new rigors. I had to learn the general orders, rank, and chain of command. I spent the rest of the training in the classroom, focusing on physical training, attention to detail, self-discipline, and teamwork. I was able to follow RDC instructions very well this time around.

I had only one issue with my training, which was swimming. I had to qualify as a third-class swimmer.

The swimming test consisted of jumping from a thirty-foot platform and swimming fifty meters, plus a five-minute prone float. I thought I knew how to swim because I used to swim back in Cameroon. I assumed that the swimming test would be an easy exercise for me because I considered myself to be a great swimmer.

Then, I experienced the jump from the thirty-foot platform. I almost drowned when I hit the water. Thank God there was a lifeguard there for those who struggled in the water. They came to my rescue as soon as they saw me struggling.

So I failed my first try miserably, and it took me about four weeks of intense swimming training to pass my swimming test. I successfully completed my swimming and my basic training, and I finally graduated from boot camp. I had to move next door for fireman training since it was my career of choice. So I had to spend another three months at Great Lakes for fireman training.

CHAPTER 22

Military Fireman Training

The fireman enlistment gave me the option to qualify for one of many engineering careers. After I graduated, I had the opportunity to choose an electrical or power plant/cogeneration plant operator, diesel mechanic, or electronics repair technician career. The goal of the training was to expose me to all those career options.

The training was mostly done in a classroom and ship environment so I could be exposed to the shipboard operations and evolutions' fundamental skills. This included stand underway engine room watches and how to maintain operating analog, work with complex machinery, maintenance, repair equipment in preparation for underway operations, observe safety standards, take part in the underway replenishment, work with qualified personnel to gain experience, operate electrical communication systems, and serve as a member of damage control, emergency, and rescue teams.

After a long three months of basic fireman training and crazy cool weather, I finally graduated from all training in May 2003. All firemen who completed the training were assigned to command, and I was assigned to a ship, the *USS Normandy*, stationed in Norfolk Naval Base in Virginia.

I packed my belongings and flew to Virginia, where I checked in to my new command. I was assigned to a fireman department. I was also assigned a bed because I was going to live onboard the ship, something I had never done before.

After I completed the check-in process, I took three weeks of a break to travel to Cameroon with two objectives in mind: to see the captain who had scammed me and to get married.

Trust me. The three-week break was fun.

CHAPTER 23

Arranged Marriage

My wife's childhood was like my childhood, with the exception that she was not physically and emotionally abused by her parents. But she went through a lot as a child living in a house with twenty people. She had six siblings, and the rest of the household was mostly her father's side of the family.

Her mother treated everyone the same, with no difference or complaisance. There was a lot of drama because mingling with twenty people in a house could have mental side effects.

This drama created an environment of distrust between distant family and my wife. She felt a little neglected because no attention was given to her by those living in the house, so she learned early how to take care of herself, how to fish, and how to be independent. She found the Lord when she was still in middle school, and

He helped her leave behind all the childhood issues, like the bullying she had gone through.

A little story about our arranged marriage. I traveled to America in 2002, and a year later, I decided to get married. I called my spiritual father, a man named Rene, back in Cameroon, and I asked him to help me find a wife. I did not want to do it myself because I knew I would be easily moved by the physical only instead of focusing on the spiritual side of a wife. Loving God with all her heart was the most important criterion I was looking for in a woman.

My spiritual father prayed, and a few months later, he had an answer from God. This was how it happened.

On his way to his store one day, Rene heard God reveal to him that a young woman he had seen visiting one of his employees at the store was the one for me.

As soon as he got to the store, he asked his employee to tell him a little more about the woman. When he received a good spiritual report about her, he wanted to see her. He requested discretion from his employee and an opportunity to meet with the woman. The employee was able to contact her and had her meet with my spiritual father.

When they met, he was impressed by her love for God and her belief. After talking for some time, he was convinced that she was rooted in the knowledge of God and that she met the requirement I had mentioned. He asked to have a picture of her via his employee so he could send it to me in the United States of America.

My requirement was nothing but the fear of God.

When I received the picture, I noticed that only her body from the waist up could be seen. It was difficult to tell if she had legs or not. After I analyzed and looked at the picture very well, I came up with some questions for my spiritual father.

One of the questions was, "Does she have legs?"

He said, "Yes," and sent more pictures of her, amongst pictures of other young women, to give me more options to choose from.

After a few months of praying, I trusted his judgment and asked him to contact the first woman, who was the one I had been confused about, so he could introduce me. Her name was Rachel.

At that point, he introduced me to her as a friend who wanted to know her. That was the first time I spoke with Rachel, and things moved quickly.

I started the conversation by being honest, and I asked her to be my friend. I laid down my entire spiritual life—when I became a Christian and the challenges I faced as one. Among other things, I mentioned that I had a daughter, whose name was Rachel as well.

According to Rachel, the fact that I was honest and shared all my ups and downs in my walk with Christ marked her trust in me and made her feel confident.

From that point on, we spoke every day about everything to try to get to know each other.

The plan was to get to know her better, even though we had not met in person. After months of talking, I had not proposed to her, and she did not have any idea what was going on or the reason behind my friendship. She suspected that I might have another plan besides friendship. At this point, she decided to get to the bottom of things.

So she went to my spiritual father to ask him, "Why this sudden friendship? How long will it last? Why does he want to be my friend?"

My spiritual father told her to ask me those questions directly.

She asked me, and I told her the reason behind my friendship, which was to know her and ask for her hand in marriage. I asked her to buy a bouquet of flowers and told her I would call her on Sunday after church to propose to her. She went and did so.

On Sunday, I called her and proposed to her. She did not give me a response that day. As a matter of fact, she asked for time to pray about it.

I would find out later that she really did not want to have anything to do with me after having seen my picture.

After months of praying, she told me that she would give me my answer when we met face to face. I let her know I was going to be in Cameroon by the end of April or late May 2003.

She shared her story with her spiritual mother and pastor's wife. They prayed about it. According to her, she was not interested in me, but something made her change her mind.

She said she received a revelation from God, which was in 1 Samuel 16:7 (NIV), "But the Lord said to Samuel, 'Do not consider his appearance or his height, for I have rejected him. The Lord does not look at the things people look at. People look at the outward appearance, but the Lord looks at the heart.'"

She decided to obey and trust God. As they continued to pray, they needed God to confirm.

So she told God about two possibilities, "First, if this matter is Your will, allow my future husband to come no later than June, as he said. And second, if he postpones his travel after June, that would be a sign to not marry him."

I kept my promise. By the end of May, I was in Cameroon. It was a confirmation that God had approved this relationship, according to Rachel.

Following confirmation from God, the ladies with whom she was praying told her it was a done deal, and they asked her to go ahead and inform her pastor, which she did. She also informed her dad and her closest family. According to Rachel, her dad did not take it very well. Her pastor also informed the church about a wedding that would take place very soon.

When I arrived in Cameroon on May 20, she was among the family members who picked me up at the airport. As soon as I got into the car, I wondered what was going on in her mind. This was the first time we had met in person, and we had the chance to know each other even more while we were driving home.

She said that in person, I was not bad at all. As for me, I found her very attractive. We decided to give it a try because we knew God was on our side.

After a while, she agreed to marry me.

She spent the night at the home of a sister in Christ because she could not spend the night at our house. It would have given a wrong perception or impression to children of God. We were prohibited from having sex before marriage, and I did not want to be a stumbling block for any child of God.

We met the next morning, and I introduced her to my family and, later on, to my church leaders. After the introduction, both families met to have a traditional marriage. Traditional marriage consisted of a ceremony during which a price for the bride was negotiated between the two families, but I also went around and met with aunts and uncles to shower them with gifts to ease the process.

My future wife's family was careful not to ask too much because the bride's price was symbolic. After my wife's price was agreed upon at the traditional wedding, four different women were brought in with their heads covered. I paid a fine every time I picked the wrong woman until I found my Rachel. This cheerful exchange went for a while, but everybody erupted into wild celebration once I got my woman.

The fun part of the ceremony was the engagement between the bride's and groom's families and friends. It took the form of entertainment, bargains, and the spray of money, all designed to keep a joyful atmosphere.

After the ceremony was over, the bride was escorted into my family's home by her aunts and cousins, and she was welcomed by my family.

Since I did not have the time to go through the normal thirty-day registration process before marriage, we went straight to see the agent in charge to explain our situation. My time in Cameroon was getting shorter, and I wanted to get married before I flew back to the US. He was gracious enough to expedite our registration into the registry for us to go ahead and do our civil marriage.

We did our civil marriage, and we got married in my church as well, and it was one of my best days ever.

Between meeting Rachel and presenting her to my family and doing the wedding, I somehow found time to go see the captain to give him a piece of my mind. It looked like everything I wanted in life was given to me by the Lord Jesus, but He wanted to show me how His revenge looked like as well.

If Joseph's brothers could have run when Joseph revealed himself to them, they would have done so in a heartbeat because they were ashamed of what they had done. In my case, it was the captain who would run.

CHAPTER 24

God's Revenge

One of my objectives during my vacation was to contact the captain. I could not believe how I had let myself be scammed by him. He took a lot of money from me by pretending to help me join the military in Cameroon, even though the Lord showed me some early scam signs in the process. But my encounter with him would serve the Lord's own purpose because He would use the entire situation for His glory.

On my first night back in Cameroon, after meeting Rachel and getting her to agree to marry me, I worked on how to see the captain the next morning. My plan was to confront him with all I knew about his scheme and how he had lied to me during my attempt to join the Cameroonian military.

To tell the truth, I did not have a good night because I could still see all the events I had gone through with the captain, and I wanted to see him have some answers to my questions. This could help me find a sense of peace within myself because I had been tormented for years by what the captain had done to me.

I did not know that Thomas, my friend who had put me in contact with the captain in the first place, knew that I had gone to the US and joined the military and that he had informed the captain.

I contacted Thomas early in the morning to find out where I could find the captain because military personnel moved around a lot. He told me the captain had not changed bases and was still in the Bonajo's base, where he was when I left.

The Holy Spirit of God was talking to me about seeking any type of revanche, but I was not listening because I wanted to have some type of revenge or holy revenge with no shotgun involved.

I called a cab early that morning when I finished with the family and headed to the captain's base to meet him to discharge all my years of frustration and anger. I wanted to make him pay for all the wrongs he had done to me and somehow get some of my money back. I was dressed in the US military uniform like I was going to war. I did not care if it was legal or not to wear an American military uniform in Cameroon.

I wanted to scare the captain, and I even wished he would pee in his pants when he saw me. In the meantime, the Lord kept reminding me that the battle was not against the flesh but against the evil spirit.

The good thing was that on my way to the captain's office, the Lord used a scary, loving tactic to soften my heart. He took me through all types of scenarios that could happen, and the outcomes of all those scenarios were not good for me and my future. By the time I got there, I had already submitted myself under God's authority and wisdom. I got to the gate, which was not far from his office, and introduced myself to the guard on duty. I asked if I could meet the captain, and the guard said yes.

The guard went to the captain's office to announce that there was a United States of America military personnel in uniform by the name of Mr. Nana out there who wanted to see him. It took a while for the guard to come back outside, but to my surprise, he came out and told me the captain had used his office window to escape. The guard was being honest with me because the captain had asked him to tell me he was not in the office.

Even though the Lord was with me all this time, there was still a war waging in my soul about forgiving and praying for the captain. You would think I would know better than to listen to the enemy's voice. So I was not fooling God by saying the captain was forgiven, but I was fooling myself. It was true that I was deceived because I was going to go back to the US without reaching my objective, but as I thought about the whole situation and the grudge I had against the captain, I realized it was not healthy to remain in that posture. I came to the conclusion that revenge was not mine but the Lord's.

Deuteronomy 32:35 (NLT) says, "It is mine to avenge; I will repay. In due time their feet will slip; their day of disaster is near and their doom rushes upon them."

I was just an enlisted man in the United States military, but I was able to make a captain of the Cameroonian army run through his office window to avoid seeing or meeting me. God's revenge was off the charts. Believe me, I did not like the fact that the captain used the window to escape because he could have hurt himself, but I could not do anything to prevent what happened. I just wanted the con artist to know that even though he meant evil, the Lord meant good. I can now clearly say that running from me was the Lord's revenge in action, but back then, I was too blind to see it.

The captain ran, and he is still running today. He was and still is living in fear because I tried multiple times to meet him but in vain. Instead of me joining the Cameroonian military, God elevated me by giving me the grace to join the most powerful military force in the entire world to confuse my enemies. I had experienced living in fear before, and it was not a good thing for me, and I believed it was and still is not good for the captain.

It was not for me to wage a war on people who had wronged me but to bring my petition to God and let Him handle it. As I freed myself from bondage, the love of God moved His way through me, and I felt very bad for the captain because living in fear was going to be a long journey for him.

Also, I did not understand that God was growing me in status in life to confuse all my enemies, not to try to get revenge for anything. The captain was not the only person who had done me wrong because a lot of people in my neighborhood had professed that my life would be a failure. They had mocked me, and they even professed I would be nobody in life. They were also confused by the grace of God in my life.

At one point, I believed those lies, and I thought I would not be able to make it in life just like they said, given my deprived situation back then. However, I learned that God was the only person holding my future. Since I gave my life to Him, He guarded me, blessed me, and made sure the plan He'd had for me since I was in my mother's womb would come to pass. Whoever had mocked me would be confused.

I learned not to lean on my own understanding. In Proverbs 3:5-6 (ESV), the Lord said, "Trust in the Lord with all your heart and do not lean on your own understanding. In all your ways acknowledge him, and he will make straight your paths."

I felt a sense of peace after I had the conversation of revenge with the Lord Jesus. I passed through my old neighborhood with my United States military uniform on, people noticed, and they looked at me like an angel coming straight from heaven. The stone that was once rejected became the cornerstone. The comment in the neighborhood was that I did not just go to the United States, but I also joined the military, which was something they could not comprehend. I became a very important man in the neighborhood.

In Matthew 21:42 (NLV), the Lord said, "The Stone that was put aside by the workmen has become the most important Stone in the building? The Lord has done this. We think it is."

I learned there was a reason behind everything I went through, and it was for God to glorify Himself in my life. Since He loved me, and I loved and trusted Him, He had turned every single evil situation done against me into good. The Lord was always ready to change my life for the better, but most of the time, I did not let Him do so because I did not surrender my entire life to Him. The Lord was in the business of confusing my enemies. I finally chose to obey the Lord for peace of mind and for my joy to be restored.

The Lord never ignored any of my prayers, and He was always working behind the scenes to make my life and joy perfect. After showing up and having a Cameroonian army captain run through the window, which was not necessary, I scheduled my return to the United States of America. I was returning with a peaceful mind because I saw God in action, and I was even more sorry for the captain.

I did not see the captain, which was one of my objectives, but I got married to a beautiful woman named Rachel.

Before leaving for the US, I really wanted to talk to the captain to let him know it was okay not to run or be afraid, and I also tried to let him know he was forgiven, but I could not find him. I even talked to his brother, Thomas, to let him know that everything was fine between us.

The Lord said in the Bible, "To me be the vengeance." I didn't quite understand what He was talking about. My own vengeance may have brought about some temporary satisfaction but would not really resolve anything, or it may have brought more distress in my life, something I did not want.

I enjoyed myself in Cameroon; I left Rachel with my mom, and I packed my stuff for the US.

Joseph and his brothers were able to come to peace and put their hate story behind them. I was not successful in coming to peace with the captain like I did with Judah.

Instead of seeking revenge, I could have just commanded my affair to the Lord like Joseph because he trusted the Lord such that he did not even try to defend himself or try to give an account of what had happened in the room with Potiphar's wife.

CHAPTER 25

Life in the US Military

I returned to the US after three weeks of vacation, which was concentrated on getting married and, especially, on making the captain's life miserable. In the process, the Lord healed my heart, and I took a loving direction.

The next day, I reported back on my ship, the *USS Normandy*. This was a Ticonderoga-class guided-missile cruiser with approximately three to four hundred officers and enlisted personnel on board. It was time to put into practice everything I had been trained to do as a fireman apprentice.

The ship had a diverse crew, Black, White, Spanish, Chinese, etc. This was going to be my new work and living environment for four years until I moved to a new duty station. I quickly acclimated myself to the new environment because my leadership took me under their wing, and they helped me familiarize myself with the ship.

I worked with the firemen department for the first two years. I was exposed to all types of duties, from academic to training to eventual sea tour assignments.

On a ship like the *USS Normandy*, my responsibility was specific. Our department's machine mate focused on duties such as maintaining the ship engine, testing, monitoring, fixing, and replacing electrical elements of any system that was broken. With all the work I had to accomplish on the ship, life was still a near boring lifestyle saturated with stress, dismay, anger, and a lot of strange things that just became a part of my day on the ship. I learned to live with people who were completely different from me in belief, color, and culture.

In the midst of different cultures, I learned that there was more than one way of thinking and no one way was better than another, except the way to Jesus, and it helped me become a better sailor, person, and follower of Christ. I always knew what I wanted from the military, which was career experience, service, and education for my future, in case I was not going to make the military a career.

My contract stipulated that after two years of fireman duty, I would have the right to choose any career I wanted if I was not satisfied with the fireman job.

Firemen on the ship were nothing compared to civilian firemen. It is true that we could fight fires, but it was more than that. I finished my two years, and I did not want to be a fireman any longer. It was time for me to choose a new career. I was a US citizen, but I was still limited in my career choices because Seabee and IT had another requirement I was not aware of. The additional requirement was that both parents had to be US citizens as well.

My career counselor suggested a few careers: electric mate, machinist's mate, and religious program specialist. The electric mate rate was closed. One down, two to go. I did not have any desire to become a machinist's mate because it was just like being a fireman, so I went for a religious program specialist.

I believed the circumstances beyond my control led me to be a religious program specialist, and it was one of the best decisions I ever made in my life. My duty as a religious program specialist on the ship consisted of serving God, the chaplain, and the country, providing support to the chaplain in his daily tasks, such as creating devotional material, helping the chaplain develop needed programs for sailors and their families, organizing faith-based events, and serving as security for the chaplain overseas. Only the US Navy has the art and the skill to transform a technician sailor into an administrator. I was the right candidate for the job because my way of life and my love for the Lord helped me to gain some respect among my peers.

Since my life reflected the love of God as best as it could, I became a source of curiosity. Most people on the ship wanted to know me, and I used the opportunity to tell my shipmates about the Lord Jesus' love and forgiveness. So everyone on the ship, from the top leadership down to the sailors, knew the values I stood for because I was living intentionally, and my words matched my behaviors.

God gave me the grace to find favor in front of the ship's leadership. I was not loved by everybody, but I did get my message across. Respect was mutual. I appreciated the respect everyone on the ship gave me by not watching adult movies when I was in the lounge room with them. I believed the Lord put me on the ship for a reason: to use the opportunity to advance the kingdom of Christ.

Our faith is revealed by our works.

Our love is revealed by our actions and how we love others.

Our obedience to the Lord's command revealed our love for him.

Rachel joined me in the US in 2004 while I was still on the ship. We managed to have an apartment in Norfolk. However, she could not speak English well, and she had to learn. Unfortunately, I would not be there to help her with basic needs like shopping or teaching her how to drive to gain her freedom.

A couple of months after her arrival, the ship was deployed for six months in the Persian Gulf. This was a very tough situation for my wife and me. I wondered how she was going to take care of herself, and on top of that, she was already three weeks pregnant.

The Navy was very organized when it came to deployment. They had mechanisms in place to help a family member get in contact with a sailor on the ship. Those mechanisms included a contact person whose primary job was to serve as a liaison between the sailor or ship and family members. They were called ombudsmen.

I inquired for the name and phone number of the ombudsman, and they were given to me. It was for me to contact her or him to set up an appointment to introduce my wife and communicate the required services Rachel would need once I was gone. I made the phone call, and I was comforted to hear a woman's voice at the other end of the line. It would not have been possible for me to leave Rachel in the care of a man.

We met, and I told her my story and gave her a list of all the services Rachel would need. This included being her personal driver to the store and to medical appointments and helping her with anything that would come up. My case was exceptional, and it was going to be a challenge to the ombudsman to take care of my wife. I

believed this woman was going to be overwhelmed because I did not think we had more than one ombudsman, and there were at least three hundred and fifty
sailors on the ship who would need her assistance.

Rachel and I prayed for me to stay behind, but the
Lord did not answer our prayer as we wanted. I worked
hard, using any means possible not to deploy. The leadership of my ship did not care when I explained my situation to them, and no matter which reasons I brought
forward to stay behind, they would not let me. They
thought I was lying or that my story did not have any
merit because sailors in the past were deceitful in telling false stories to get out of deployment.

I was constrained to deploy in February 2005, no
matter the effort I put in to stay behind and take care of
my wife. Our deployment was mainly for training with
regional and coalition partners, to provide naval avia-
tion support, and to deter any tension by our obvious
presence in the Gulf.

On our way to the Persian Gulf, we made some stops
in different countries like Spain, Malta, and Greece.
The location that got my attention was the island of
Malta because it was a historic place in the Bible where
Paul was bitten by a poisonous snake but did not suffer
any ill effects. It was meaningful for me to visit Malta
because there were a lot of places visited by Jesus, Paul,
and other disciples I had never actually visited. It was a

life-changing event for me. God helped me to connect the dots, and I was lucky to have the experience.

However, I could not really enjoy myself because I was worried about my wife. I used a phone line to call her from Malta.

To my surprise, she said, "The ombudsman invited me to her church because she knew we were a Christian family."

The Sunday after my departure, the ombudsman picked Rachel up for church. Jesus had everything planned for my wife because when she got to the church, she met a lady by the name of Lynda Carrington, and she took Rachel under her wing and became her personal chauffeur.

She took Rachel to grocery stores and medical appointments and kept her company. Mrs. Lynda was a businesswoman who loved the Lord, and her encounter with Rachel was nothing but a miracle and a providence from the Lord. She just loved my wife, and the two have a mother-daughter relationship to this day.

Mrs. Lynda adopted my wife as her own daughter and introduced her to American society. Rachel would soon find out she was a people person while spending time with her.

Mrs. Lynda had adopted a lot of needy children in the past, and she was always reaching out to people in need. She taught Rachel how to shop for the baby's needs, and she was there every step of the pregnancy. Lynda's husband was also a gentleman. He taught Rachel how to drive. I was very happy when Rachel gave me good news, and a heavy burden was lifted from my heart.

After Malta, we visited more countries, but our main goal was to stay in the Persian Gulf.

Contact between Rachel and I was constant. I updated her on every stop or country we visited, and she gave me updates on her situation and all the help she was getting from Mrs. Lynda.

Almost six months into the deployment, I got a phone call from my wife. She had just given birth to a baby girl. Our first daughter was born on September 1, 2005.

My commanders knew about the birth of my daughter, and they flew me back home. I reunited with my family, and I met Mrs. Lynda for the first time.

When I returned from my deployment, my baby was one month old, and I suddenly had a large family, whom I thanked God for. I thanked Mrs. Lynda for being a blessing to our family and for all the support she gave to Rachel during my deployment. I resumed my life with Rachel and my first daughter, whom we named Amarissa.

CHAPTER 26

Boots on
the Ground
Deployment

Down the road, we had another beautiful girl, Raya, in September 2007. Unlike Amarissa, Raya had meningitis a month after her birth, and it scared Rachel and me. We even thought we were going to lose our baby. Rachel and I spent weeks at the hospital for her treatment.

I was scheduled to go to Iraq as an Individual Mobilization Augmentee deployment to support the Iraq freedom mission in November 2007. This time, it was boots on the ground. With my daughter hospitalized, I started the process of getting out of the deployment because I was not sure if she would get well before I deployed. But I was not successful this time either.

There was not as much panic this time as there had been with the first deployment because I knew Rachel would have the support she would need from Mrs. Lynda. We were a family at this point. I was lucky because my daughter got well a week before I left for Iraq.

For Navy personnel to deploy to Iraq, they had to go through the Army basic training at Fort Dix MEPS New Jersey because it was a battleground deployment that required every person to know all about combat. In November 2007, all selectees rode a bus to Fort Dix for basic training. As soon as we got there, we had a briefing on how to navigate the base and where to find different stores. Since it was late at night, they had to show us our dormitory so we could spend the night and be ready for the next morning. The Army has rules when it comes to where the men and women should spend the night. Men and women had different and separate dormitories. This was true for every branch of the military.

I'd had problems since I immigrated to the United States of America. People always assumed I was a girl based on my first name. In the French language, both boys and girls could be named Desire(e) as a first name. Boys are "Desire" with one "e," and girls are "Desiree" with the double "e." I quite understood the confusion here in the United States of America because it is not a French-speaking country.

It was time to go to bed to get refreshed for the next morning. I went to look for my dormitory.

The names were displayed on every room's door to make it easy for personnel to find their respective dormitory. I found my name on a door and assumed it was my dormitory.

I was the first one inside, but a couple of minutes after I went in, a bunch of women entered as well. They started to get undressed, and as a child of God, I could not let that happen.

I said, "Excuse me! There is a man in the room."

Every woman turned and looked at me like I was a monster. There was panic everywhere in the room as soon as they heard a man's voice and saw me.

They shouted, "Intruder!"

I thanked the Lord that none of them had taken off their pants because I would have passed out. I just knew there had been a mistake and that somebody had put my name on the wrong door.

I grabbed all my belongings and went to the administration office to be reassigned to the men's dormitory.

The first week was classroom training, which included basic first aid, sexual harassment and assault awareness and prevention, chemical radioactive biological and nuclear readiness, and the proper usage of breathing masks in the war zone and navigation course.

The second week, I trained on my assigned primary weapon. We also had training on the basics of rifle marksmanship, rifle maintenance, and how to engage targets at varying distances. Also, how to prioritize multiple targets simultaneously, training on advanced machine guns like M9 and M4, and how to throw a grenade. We also learned convoy operation, engaging targets as part of the team, and identifying and disabling individual explosive device techniques.

The last week of training focused more on practice, which included a multiple-day land navigation practice to test our survival, fitness, vehicle roll-over training, day and night land navigation, field active live shooting target, and many more things.

One of my duties in the war zone as a religious program specialist was to protect the Navy chaplain at all costs. For this reason, the chaplain made me carry two weapons—an M16 and a 9NM—instead of one weapon. He was concerned with my shooting skills, and the 9NM was to be used by the chaplain in case he may need it, but he was banned from carrying a weapon.

The training finished with a series of tests to assess our ability to react against an enemy force on the battlefield and how to work as a team to win the battle. Once all was said and done, we gathered our equipment, and a flight was arranged for Kuwait, which was close to the theater of operations where we could familiarize ourselves with the area before we could be sent to the command to be part of the war in Iraq. After two weeks of zone familiarization, we flew to Iraq.

As soon as I got there, the chaplain took command of the church and assumed the Sunday worship, daily confidential counseling, performing religious rites, and advising commanders on religious, spiritual, and moral matters. I assumed and coordinated chaplain protection. I established a religious support operation, such as recordkeeping and management of all religious programs.

I recall many incidents where rockets were launched at our base, but they were all unsuccessful and did not cause any major damage. But it created a sense of fear in the chaplain and me.

One day, the chaplain and I were supposed to leave the base to visit a nearby Iraqi children's school to give them some school supplies. But the chaplain did not let me participate because, once again, he was not confident in my shooting skills, so he chose a sniper instead of me.

Other than that, every day was the same routine, which was to eat, do our duty, and do firearm shooting practice. Heart pounding, fear of the unknown, anxiety, and tunnel vision were also part of my daily routine.

I had the chance to communicate daily with my family back home, so I could know about my daughter

Raya's recovery. I was updated on her health progress every day.

We learned after six months that we were going home in May 2008, and I was so excited to go back to Rachel and the children and finish a chapter of my life. We had gone to Iraq as a group, and we were coming back as a group because a new group was going to take over once we left.

I spent more than seven months in Iraq, and I finally came home.

After a short break at home, I was back on deployment again.

Deployment and my absence created a lot of stress in my family. I had two children, and Rachel had to play my role in addition to her own. It was a long stretch for my spouse. I found out my little Raya could not even recognize me because when I was back home from a deployment, she called me "uncle" and broke my heart. I resolved to get out of the military and be a civilian.

It was easier said than done because I would stay in the Navy until August 21, 2011, when I would finally put the gun down and get out of the military for my children and my wife's well-being and begin my civilian career.

Life in the military was very challenging, especially with all the stress that I went through, which took a toll on my health. In addition to my involvement in a combat zone, I got out of the service with disabled veteran status.

I was lucky Raya was still a kid, and I could make up for the lost time. All this was to testify to the goodness of God in allowing me to join the military and do what I had always wanted.

The Lord was always watching over my family and me like He watched over Jacob and his sons when Joseph was in Egypt.

CHAPTER 27

American Dream

I was the laughingstock of everyone around my neighborhood in Cameroon, and some of my friends judged me based on my previous life's condition. But I always told them I serve a living God, and He holds my future in His hand. It did not matter what they saw now because God had a plan for my life.

Working hard was part of most African cultures because it was the only way you could make it in life if you were lucky. African countries did not provide aid to their people. It was very difficult to find an African who had immigrated to the US on the street looking for a handout.

Most of us came to the United States to better our life. The only way was to go to school because we were taught when we were growing up that education could help change one's life.

When I came back from my first deployment in 2005, Rachel and I started school. Rachel was careful to choose the right school. She did not want to spend years educating herself and not find suitable employment because of her strong French accent.

After some research, I convinced her to go with nursing. Speaking the English language fluently was not enforced in nursing recruitment like the other fields. She chose the Tidewater community, and I chose Saint Leo University online for a national security program since I was building up experience in the military.

We did not have any family close by who could help us with our little girl, Amarissa, whom Rachel was still breastfeeding. I took my daughter to the daycare in the morning with frozen breastmilk that Rachel had extracted the night before and kept in the freezer for the baby to drink during the day. I had to pick her up on my way back home around four thirty.

Rachel breastfed her as soon as we got home every day, and I would then drive Rachel to school. The classes were from six to 10 p.m., and since she was breastfeeding every hour, I had to drive back and forth every hour for her to feed our baby. Amarissa refused to take anything else except her mom's breast milk. We did that for almost a year until Rachel stopped breastfeeding her. But I drove Rachel to school until she got a driver's license.

Rachel took a placement test before starting school to determine her English level and was placed in a program called ESL, or English as a Second Language, before starting her English 101 and then her nursing program.

The placement test was not an issue for me since I had already taken a lot of English courses while in basic training in the military. That gave me a good foundation, so after the test, I was placed directly into English 101 and into a bachelor's program. It took me four years to complete my bachelor's and two years to complete my master's degree while I was still in the military. Rachel was resolved to finish her nursing program even though it was tough, and she almost quit at one point. After she completed two years of ESL, she then successfully completed her bachelor's in four years and her master's degree in two years as well. We did our best during my military deployment, raising our children and going to school because we were determined to accomplish the American dream.

I still remember when we had our second child, Raya, who was diagnosed with meningitis just a month after her birth. Rachel and I spent our time at the hospital taking care of our daughter and studying.

Even when I deployed the second time to Iraq, I was taking the course online since I had access to the internet. The military vocational rehabilitation counselor gave me a laptop to use for my school in Iraq. I used my time in Iraq very wisely by taking online classes while I was there.

My combat buddies would ask me how I did it. After an exhausting day of work, I still had time and energy to do online schoolwork. My response to them was that I had set a priority for my life and committed to it.

I had a similar question with my friends on the ship, but it was just a little different. My friends and I were talking mostly about our future after we left the military. Our goal was to do eight years max in the military and get out to pursue a civilian career. Going to school to get a degree was one way for us to get ready for the outside world. Since I was in school already, I asked them to sign up for school as well so we would all be ready for the outside world

But none of them would sign up for school because, according to one friend, "You do not have any life when you take evening classes because it takes away your fun time."

But I always told them I would be able to have a life once I finished school. I got my degree and any certificates I could have before I got out, but as for my friends, they got out with zero degrees or certificates. Most of them went back to what they had done before joining the military.

While I was in the military, I could take as many classes as I could because tuition and books were free, so I took the opportunity and sacrificed my fun time to offer myself a path for a successful life after the military. But my friends did not see life as I saw it, and they did not even keep their promise to go to school once they left the military.

The military offered a certificate as well, and all you needed to do was to register in the program online and log in your working hours. When you reached a certain number of hours, they gave you a certificate. A lot of sailors did not even take advantage of that program.

I'm not saying everybody on the ship was like my friends who did not want to have an education before they got out of the military. There were a lot of sailors on the ship who took the opportunity for free education and support to get educated, even if they were planning to stay until they retired. I'm just saying it was necessary, especially for those who were planning to be prepared for the outside world, which was not easy.

The Lord wants us to always prepare ourselves for the next challenge in our life, especially when He has given us a heads-up. In Joseph's case, it was in a dream. In mine, it was through promises and prophecy.

CHAPTER 28

Spiritual Complacency in the US

I lived in Maryland for six months. There, I failed two military entry exams. I moved to Georgia, where I finally passed my entrance exam and joined the military, and I stayed there for four months. I left Georgia for Great Lakes, Illinois, for military training (boot camp), and I finally moved to Virginia when I completed my basic military training. I stayed in Virginia for all my military service and career.

The moves created a sense of instability in my spiritual life. Life was easier in America, and I became complacent because it required only a small effort on my part to have all I wanted compared to Cameroon, where determination and great effort to get a job were required. I barely had one meal a day in Cameroon, but in the US, I found myself with an embarrassment of choices of what to eat.

In Cameroon, I prayed for meals, but not in the US, and this was true for other needs as well.

My daily routine in Cameroon included prayer, Bible reading, and practice. But in the US, after some time, my worship and routine started to fade away. I started to lean on my own understanding, and I was losing my first love for Christ. Plus, I was not successful in finding a home church like my home church in Cameroon. I did not have peer group support where I could be spiritually fed and stay connected to God, so the voice of God became distant. The enemy's voice filled my head.

Reading my Bible became just a routine practice, and it did not mean that much to me anymore, even though I knew the importance of daily Bible reading for my soul. I might die if I do not eat to feed my flesh, and the same thing is true for me when I do not read the Word of God as food to feed my soul and spirit. I started to die spiritually because I was distant from God.

Matthew 4:4 (KJV) states, "But he answered and said, It is written, Man shall not live by bread alone, but by every word that proceedeth out of the mouth of God."

I still remember when I was faithful in reading the Word of God and praying every morning and when the Word of God was written on my heart. I felt connected to God, and reading helped set the course of my day. The Spirit in me helped me meditate, and it also helped with my reading and staying in prayer most of the day. Sometimes, my daily meditation brought forward in my heart songs of worship. This habit prevented my mind from wandering and created a sense of a pure mind and soul.

When I lived a careless life, no discipline, no boundaries, no Bible reading, I went back to my vomit. Dogs have this nasty habit of going back to their vomit. I kind of behaved like a dog by doing what I used to do and repeating things—like telling lies or feeling pride, greed, lust, and anger—that I had entered into a covenant with the Lord not to do again. I found myself helpless. My prayers became weak, and I could no longer feel a connection with the Lord. I dropped to a lower level of moral standards because I was no longer focusing on God's love and His Word.

My heart changed from loving the things of God to the things of the world. I desired to make a lot of money and impress people around me, especially those who had done me wrong by calling me names and saying I would not be anything in life. I tried to fool myself and God by believing the money I sought was to help the poor, orphans, and all those in need. Making money is not a bad thing, but it was an issue because I started to be more concerned about money rather than the things of God. In the process, I quenched the Holy Spirit's voice in me.

Jesus said it would be very difficult for a rich man to go to heaven because of the risk of trusting in your wealth rather than in God.

The Lord warned the children of Israel not to break their covenant once they entered the Promised Land, where they would be blessed beyond measure.

As for me, I did not have a formal warning from the Lord about how to live once I was in the United States of America because God expected me to live as a child of God no matter which country I found myself in.

We know that Joseph stayed faithful to God in Egypt because we have an account of him running away from adultery.

As for me, not so much because I would give in to complacency.

In Cameroon, one of my motivations to go to church was because I loved the Lord, and I wanted to serve Him. But also, I had problems in my life I wanted God to intervene in, namely my emotional and physical abuse and poverty. I believed the Lord could heal me and change my life for the better, which He did.

Like any human being, I wanted to be blessed because I did not have anything, and the Lord heard my prayer and moved me to the US. I got my priorities somehow mixed up when I came to the United States of America, just like the children of Israel. An abundant material life and the desire to make more money took precedence over my spiritual needs.

Since I was blessed with every material thing I could imagine and want, I thought my main concern in life had been answered, which was according to my flesh, and that I did not need to put forth a lot of effort to live as a Christian anymore. But I was wrong because abundance creates its own problem, which is spiritual laziness. Not all problems come from the search for money.

It would take me years to comprehend that my spiritual life was more important than material things. I could live a spiritual life without a lot of material things—just the necessities to go through life—but it was possible to own a lot of material things or have a lot of money and still be faithful to the Lord, as long as the things or money did not become an idol.

I knew I would be subjected to many blessings in the US because the word in Cameroon was that the US was the most blessed country in the entire world. This was true, but I also knew how strong my faith was in the Lord. I thought I was prepared for anything life could throw at me, but I would find out very quickly that living as a poor man and living in abundance were quite different. The poorer I was, the easier it was for me to love God and trust Him. But the more money or material I had, the more difficult it became to put my trust in Him.

Compared to Cameroon, I was very rich here in the States. I regarded the privileged life I was living in the US as success, which bred a spiritual complacency far more dangerous than failure in my life.

After years in the US, I no longer trusted and loved the Lord as I should, and I started to believe in myself. I felt a sense of entitlement instead of gratitude.

I would act just like the children of Israel when they crossed the Jordan River with Joshua to the Promised Land.

After crossing the Jordan, the children of Israel forgot all about the forty years of wilderness wandering spent in the desert and stopped following the Lord's commands. They started to live a sinful life, and as a consequence, they would suffer all types of problems that come with being disobedient to the Lord. They went through a lot of hardship.

For example, the spiritual life of Israelites began to decrease after Joshua died, and the children of Israel's sons and daughters started getting married to the Canaanites and worshiping their false gods. The children of God started perishing as a consequence.

It was true for me as well because I returned way back to Egypt by being disobedient to the covenant I had with the Lord. And the enemy used the love of money to have a hold on me. But before I knew it, I became a great actor in the world of unfaithfulness, unrighteousness, and deceit.

Because of seven years of famine, the children of God found themselves in Egypt. For the next several centuries, the Israelites were enslaved by the Egyptians, who used and abused them. Being freed by Moses after years, all they could remember were the antagonisms and suffering they went through during their stay in Egypt. The world became an antagonism and suffering place because of all the torment it possessed.

My willingness to do what was good was dominated by my desire to do evil. The Apostle Paul gave me an idea a long time ago about how to prepare for or go about spiritual battle every day, which I ignored once I got to the US.

Paul wrote in Ephesians 6:13-18 (NIV):

> Therefore, put on the full armor of God, so when the day of evil comes, you may be able to stand your ground, and after you have done everything, to stand. Stand firm then, with the belt of truth buckled around your waist, with the breastplate of righteousness in place, and with your feet fitted with the readiness that comes from the gospel of peace. In addition to all this, take up the shield of faith, with

which you can extinguish all the flaming ar-
rows of the evil one. Take the helmet of salvation and the sword of the Spirit, which is the
word of God. And pray in the Spirit on all occasions with all kinds of prayers and requests.
With this in mind, be alert and always keep on
praying for all the Lord's people.

Because the spiritual war is real, we should all be
aware because ignorance is one of the enemy tools
against us. The Lord, through the years, has taught me
some practical ways to spiritually protect myself against
enemies' attacks.

The Lord wants us to pursue the truth and make
it part of our daily life. Putting on the armor helps us
stand up to the evil. This truth could only be revealed to
me through reading the Bible every day. Reading Scripture helped me to know the will and promises of God,
which helped me resist the devil.

As for the Breastplate of Righteousness, the Lord
made me righteous on the cross, and He wanted me to
guard my heart by not exposing myself to unrighteous
behavior, such as immorality. An unguarded heart al-
lows the enemy to weaken my love and the gift of righteousness the Lord gave me.

A small group was important in my search for a home
church. I needed a brother to point out some of my

weaknesses. I desired to enjoy the gospel of peace. God just wanted me to be in peace with everyone around me, if it was possible, and to have peace wherever I went.

The Shield of Faith came by reading and hearing the Word of God to be replenished and be fully functional in my walk with Christ.

The Helmet of Salvation was the cross and the knowledge of the Word of God, which would reveal God's truth to me, and I would be able to protect my mind against the evil attack, which primarily took place in my mind. The enemy was always injecting his thoughts into my mind to make me his subject.

The Sword of the Spirit is the Word of God, and by dwelling in the Word of God, I would be defensive and offensive against any enemy attack by using the word to bring the enemy's temptation to rest once for all. The Lord wanted me to use His Word to resist the enemy so that he could fly away from me.

Prayer. The Lord always asks me to stay in prayer because the enemy is around looking to devour me. When I stopped taking the battle seriously and praying consistently, I suffered setbacks in my walk with the Lord Jesus.

People like Job in the Bible were an exception to the rich man. His riches did not distract him or turn him away from the love of God because he never loved his wealth more than God in the first place.

The Lord proved to me time after time that He was trustworthy, but my daily life experience turned into a frequent state of panic and fear. The love of the world took a heavy toll on my health, joy, and peace because I started to struggle and worry about everything in life.

It also took a toll on my family. I wasn't the spiritual leader for my children and wife. The Lord said in Philippians 4:6-7 (NLT), "...not to worry about anything; instead, pray about everything. Tell God what you need, and thank him for all he has done. Then you will experience God's peace, which exceeds anything we can understand. His peace will guard your hearts and minds as you live in Christ Jesus."

I did not apply this passage, so I was overwhelmed by worldly things. I would cast all my problems to God and then take them back a couple of minutes later because I wanted to define the outcome of the problem. The truth: the problem I had cast on the Lord did not leave my mind.

First Peter 5:7 (AMP) says, "Casting all your cares [all your anxieties, all your worries, and all your concerns, once and for all] on Him, for He cares about you [with deepest affection, and watches over you very carefully."

In my complacency, God ran after me to rescue me. I saw His saving hand in every bad situation which could have cost me.

If I had followed Joseph's faithful example and kept my covenant with the Lord or kept Joseph character traits, my life would have been rich and generally more successful in my faith, and I would have never gotten myself into a complacency mindset.

CHAPTER 29

God's Recure in My Complacence

After I left the military—before I opened my contracting business—I got a good job with the department of defense, with whom I worked for a year. My company had a disabled military veteran's designation, and I bid on the government's project under my designation.

But the business was built on the sand because I did not take the time to evaluate my capacity, success, or failure, and I did everything under emotion on the presumption that I would learn in the process because I did not have any federal contracting experience under my belt. I did not even talk to Rachel before I quit my job and did not realize that contracting with the government required a lot of paperwork, insurance, and certifications. To get a project, I needed liability insurance and a bond.

There were three main types of bonds in construction: bid, payment, and performance. Each was designed to guarantee that I would perform the job no matter what. Bid bonds guaranteed that I would perform the job at the proposed price, even if additional costs occurred during the project. Payment bonds guaranteed that I would pay any supplier and subcontractors on the job. Performance bonds guaranteed that I would perform the job.

Usually, payment and performance bonds were required conjointly. To be able to obtain a payment and performance bond from any insurance company, I had to sign a general indemnity agreement, which stipulated that if I failed to meet my obligation—such as paying my suppliers and performing and completing the project on time—the insurance company would go after me and my assets to recuperate their money. This included my home and everything I owned.

I got four contracts that I was able to perform without any issues.

Then I got a contract with the Army Corp of Engineers in Pennsylvania to renovate two bathrooms and install a new window. Everything went fine. The two bathrooms were completed, except for some touch-ups. The window was ordered, but it never came because that particular window was in high demand. Because of the window not received and installed, the government wanted to terminate the contract for default.

Termination for default meant that I was facing the prospect of being forced to return progress payments, of being liable to the government for any excess costs of re-procurement, and it was not good to have a default termination on my record. This would limit my ability to obtain additional government work. In addition, the bonding company would have evaluated the remaining costs, which was a lot of money, and come after me to get the money to finish the project.

Thank God for His grace because He heard my prayers and changed the government's previous consideration. Instead of terminating the contract by default, we just went our separate ways. They took the initiative to have someone else install the window once it arrived without any additional payment. This would have brought a great deal of financial distress upon my family and me if the Lord had not intervened.

The Lord's grace that brought me out of this situation made me rethink how I viewed the Lord's grace. At one point in my life, I felt a sense of disconnection between the Lord and me, which is normal. I thought the Lord did not hear my prayers. I also felt like my prayers did not have the necessary anointing to reach the throne of God for Him to make a move on my behalf because of my unrighteous living. I could not pray on any of God's promises in my life and reference any verse in the Bible to support my claims anymore because I had forgotten a lot of Bible verses that had been written on my heart.

Under the Old Testament, children are completely separated from the Lord when they sin. According to Isaiah 59:2 (NLT), the Lord says, "It's your sins that have cut you off from God. Because of your sins, he has turned away and will not listen anymore."

Even John said in John 9:31 (NASB), "We know that God does not listen to sinners; but if someone is God-fearing and does His will, He listens to him."

Knowing that God was still with me in the midst of struggle within my soul, flesh, and spirit between returning to the love of God and continuing to live a hopeless life started to wage a war on my health. I became depressed, and I gave up. I realized the energy I put out to reject the love of God was more than the energy to love Him.

Even tithing became a serious issue. I made my own rule for giving, which would, later on, take me off the course and the purpose of giving. At the beginning of my life in the United States of America, I was very faithful in giving my tithe to the Lord. But after a while, I started leaning on my own understanding. I decided to give my tithe according to my concept, which was to use it to help my family in Cameroon instead of giving it to a local church in the United States.

I believed that US churches had a lot of money and consequently did not deserve more. This was an unconventional way of thinking. I chose to send my tithe to my previous church in Cameroon, where I was no longer spiritually fed.

In the beginning, it made sense to send my tithe home because I was still searching for a local church. But the moment I had a new pastor and a new local church where I could praise and serve the Lord, I should have given my tithe there. I was confusing tithe with donation, and there was a war waging within my soul because I was asking myself if I was doing the right thing.

At one point, I stopped giving my tithe to the needy because, in the search of material things, I put myself in debt. Paying my debt took precedence over helping the needy, and once again, the concept looked good financially but not so much spirituality. My heart was valuing things more than God.

The enemy whispered in my heart, "After you pay tithe, you won't have enough money to cover expenses."

Paying off my obligation was an honorable thing to do, but paying my tithe should have been a priority for my spiritual life. Once again, the enemy had me where he wanted me. He was successful at distracting me and confusing me. Giving to the needy was not a bad thing for me to do. Actually, the Lord loves cheerful givers, but it would be wise to tithe first.

When I did something right, I had profound peace of mind and soul. Since the war within did not produce any peace, I concluded that it was wrong. Each time I had any fight within me about doing what was right or wrong, my physical, mental, and spiritual health suffered. I found myself sinking deeply in the water but thanked God when His unwavering love rescued me.

The Lord wanted me to pay my tithe to my local church to support the needs of the body of Christ, reach more souls, and help meet the needs of the community.

Isaiah 41:10 (ESV) says, "Fear not, for I am with you; Be not dismayed, for I am your God. I will strengthen you, Yes, I will help you, I will uphold you with My righteous right hand."

My problem was not the Lord but me because I was putting my trust in the things of the world.

Amid these trials, Rachel had no choice but to be the spiritual leader of the house, which was not acceptable. She never stopped warning me that I was on the wrong path or going astray from the Lord. Rachel was like Jacob in the sense that he probably called Joseph to stay on the right path, which was Jesus.

CHAPTER 30

Tentative Return to the Lord

Jesus is more than enough. With little love left in me for the Lord and His grace, it helped to reconnect with Him in a mighty way.

Jesus put it this way in Matthew 6:33 (NIV), "But seek first his kingdom and his righteousness, and all these things will be given to you as well."

I thanked God for His grace because He would deliver me from my miserable life.

When the need to change outweighed the need to stay the same, I started to do some self-evaluation to reconnect with the Lord. If someone asked me the question, "Why did it take you so long to renew your faith and run back to the Lord?" I would not have been able to answer them because I was in denial with myself, and I thought I was right where the Lord wanted me to be.

Just like the prodigal son, I waited until I was not able to continue to eat pig's food or continue on a destructive and unhealthy route to go back home. When I look back during moments in my life when I loved the Lord Jesus with all my heart, mind, and spirit, I was full of love, joy, and peace. I had a strong connection with the Lord, and I was also free indeed, and the enemy could not get to me that easily. But when I stopped loving the Lord, peace, joy, and everything that came with it disappeared in my life, and it became a theatre of the enemy, where he played as he pleased. I went down in depression, which prevented me from being the spiritual leader in our house as I used to be.

I went about returning to the Lord as I did with my New Year's resolution. I set goals, for example, to eat healthily and lose weight during the year. But unfortunately, I would give in one or two months into my resolution, and I would start to live a faithful life, and I would go back to the old me after a while.

As a child of God, I was supposed to be running away from sins and hate them, so why did I go back? It was because I was a slave to sin. I believe the prodigal son loved his father even more when he went through all the bad experiences away from his dad. When he finally came to his senses and went back home to his father, he did not just love his dad more, but he stayed for good, and he never left his dad again. He would still make some mistakes at home, but he was in the care of his loving father, who covered him with his love.

Thank God for His grace because I ran back to Him even though I deceived myself many times. But His love was greater than the deceitfulness.

I realized the willingness to run back to the Lord and stay with Him would not be enough, but the intention to stay and lean on God and have a real relationship with the Lord was required.

A purposeful and intentional relationship would rely on the principle of surrendering my life to Him and acknowledging what the Lord had done for me on the cross. This included defying my flesh. I had to intentionally do daily Bible study and daily prayer to have an intentional desire to become like Jesus, and above all, to learn how to cast my fear, my doubt, and my flaws upon Him once again. I needed the help of the Lord because I could not resist the evil by my own strength.

I renewed my relationship with Lord, and I started living as I was going to give an account of my life to Jesus, not for the good I have done, but for how He asked me to live. Even under His grace, I was called to live a loving, righteous, and forgiving life, which made me a prisoner.

Romans 14:12 (NIV) says, "So then, each of us will give an account of ourselves to God."

God's grace gave me the power to do His will and to be motivated not to live a sinful life. The Spirit transforms my sinful nature and heart and leads it toward godliness.

I took my spiritual battle seriously by putting on my armor every day. I also ought to live as if I were in combat because the enemy is always looking to make my life miserable. I must be vigilant in the search for Christ and not give in to my fleshly desires, like laziness. I must live as someone wanting the heaven prize.

First Corinthians 9:24 (ISV) states, "You know that in a race all the runners run but only one wins the prize, don't you? You must run in such a way that you may be victorious."

Apostle Paul himself said in 1 Corinthians 9:27 (NLV), "I keep working over my body. I make it obey me. I do this because I am afraid after I have preached the Good News to others, I myself might be put aside."

I put all my worries and life's unfortunate events upon Him, and the weight of my sin lightened. Depression and all unhealthy habits of mine faded, and my healing process began. Joy, love, and peace of mind started to settle back into my life once again. In one word, I became alive again.

This did not mean I had everything under control, but at least I was at a point where I could have an honest conversation with my God about everything. A complete return to the Lord had brought nothing but joy, peace, and love.

As for tithing, I freed myself from the different ideas I had about it and the idea that I would not be able to cover my expenses once I paid my tithe.

Even though I was not a hundred percent faithful in my giving, an act of faith brought joy and a sense of participating and belonging in something greater than myself. I had even tried to talk Rachel into the idea of using the tithe to bless people in need, and she went along with me for a while. After that, she decided to give her tithe back to her local church.

Tithing should be a personal issue because, according to the Scripture, my right hand should not know what the left hand was giving.

I started to put on my armor to wage fights against my sins to allow the Lord to come and dine with me again every day, every hour, and every minute. The connection between the Lord and me was restored, and I started to hate my old way of life.

In Ezekiel 36:31 (NIV), the Lord says, "Then you'll remember your lifestyles and practices were not good. You'll hate yourselves as you look at your own iniquities and disgusting practices."

In my life, I had the chance to experience the two extremes—poverty and plenty—on my own level. As a poor person, I wanted more. As I got more, I wanted to have more and more. The circle continues, and the pursuit of either of one those did not bring any joy into my life. On the contrary, it brought me misery, and I became captive to the idea of making it happen instead of doing my part and then letting it happen.

Making it happen was not a bad idea in itself, but it was a bad idea when I was getting absorbed by whatever I wanted to make happen. Being obsessed with making it happen had consequences. I did not know when to stop, and I became an idol for myself. I did learn life realities, which advised me to take a different path or direction because the pursuit of all things under the sun was vanity, except the pursuit of God's love, like Joseph.

CHAPTER 31

They Meant Evil, but God Used It for Good

The Lord could have changed my dad, but it would have required him to be open and ready to be changed. Instead, the Lord used my dad's evildoing, like that of Joseph's brothers, to turn it into a blessing. Even though I did not want an evildoer near me, I finally understood how he played a major role in my life because God used his evildoing to fulfill some of His plans in my life.

Romans 8:28 (NIV) states, "We know that in all things God works for the good of those who love him, who have been called according to his purpose."

The Lord turned Judah's evildoing into a blessing by using the three weeks between my firing and my rehiring to make me play the US lottery. When I moved to

Mr. Innocent's house, the last thing I expected was to become a child of God. I had resisted the idea of being a Christian for years, but the Lord knew that in order to have me on His side, I would need to experience and see the love and the word of God in action through living. Any child of God could have spent years talking to me about God, and I would not have changed anything in my belief since I had witnessed Christians using God's name in vain.

I continued to thank Jesus because He had a plan to bring me to Him, to heal me, to reconcile my family, to bless me, and to bring me to the United States of America. This happened through chaos and challenges. When I look back, I just want to worship my God, who changed water into wine, changed my tears into laughter and joy, and changed my heart of stone into a heart of flesh. As a child of God, my life would be blessed because He would open the door for me to find my first good job, to play the US lottery, and then to move to the United States of America.

The man who was once rejected became a man of the greatest importance, and the man who was once denied and scammed while attempting to join the Cameroonian Army joined the best and most powerful army in the whole world. Even though I lost my faith for a while, it would serve His own purpose by making me realize the value of reading the Word of God daily, of prayer, of paying tithe, and of being in the community of believers. I noticed children of God were instrumental in God's plan for my life, from getting my first job up to playing the lottery to traveling to the US. I wondered if God's plan in my life would have still happened in the order it happened if I were not a member of the body of Christ.

Joseph loved the Lord as well, and it was why his story in the Bible was unique in the sense that God Himself was behind the story.

My story is unique as well because the Lord is behind it all.

When I look back at my dismissal from my job, something always comes into my mind: God's timing. I mentioned that I had an issue with one of my colleagues as soon as I got to the job, but the Lord gave me the wisdom to navigate between those issues without being dismissed early. Judah was very mean to me, and he used any opportunity he had to let me know I was not welcomed and would never take his place. He wanted to be the number two in the electrical department. He also purposely undermined my leadership and backstabbed and criticized me in front of leaders just to make me look bad.

The complexity of rivalry in the workplace in Cameroon was like here in the United States of America, where people did not know their boundaries.

In Cameroon, people would go as far as to visit a marabout, who used magic, charms, and spiritual forces to seek help in eliminating the opponent.

I took my co-worker very seriously, and I did not focus on the impact of his behavior or the wrongs he was doing to me but rather focused on my own behavior to make sure that no matter what he did or how he behaved, I showed him the love of God. The Lord used me to show His love, patience, kindness, goodness, faithfulness, gentleness, and self-control around the workplace. The Lord asked me to love my enemy.

> Do not repay anyone evil for evil. Be careful to do what is right in the eyes of everyone. If it is possible, as far as it depends on you, live at peace with everyone. Do not take revenge, my dear friends, but leave room for God's wrath, for it is written: "It is mine to avenge; I will repay," says the Lord. On the contrary: "If your enemy is hungry, feed him; if he is thirsty, give him something to drink. In doing this, you will heap burning coals on his head."
>
> Romans 12:17-21 (NIV)

The Lord wanted me to love Judah. I was someone's enemy at some point, and I had enemies in my life, but the Lord saved me, and I was in the position to understand the evildoing of Judah because it was not Judah but the enemy behind him. A sincere prayer for him made me realize that the physical man in front of me was not the person to blame but the evil spirit behind him controlling him.

Ephesians 6:12 (KJV) says, "For we wrestle not against flesh and blood, but against principalities, against powers, against the rulers of the darkness of this world, against spiritual wickedness in high places."

The Lord called me to do things out of the ordinary, like being kind to my enemies by overcoming evil with good, avoiding strife, forgiving even if I thought that the other person should ask for forgiveness first, and trusting in the Lord, having faith—not fear or dismay—in the midst of adversity. Because the Lord is always with me, I must love and pray for people who bully me and do not love me.

I visited my enemy at the hospital. I did to others what I would like to have done to me because if I acted ordinary, there would not be any difference between me—a child of God—and a non-believer.

It was very difficult to hate those I sincerely prayed for. My opponent at the job was looking to get physical, but I never gave him an opportunity, and sometimes I wondered what would have happened if I had lost my self-control and gotten into a fight. I would have gotten fired or worse. Would God's plan for my life to go to the United States of America still have happened in the same order or at all? What if Jesus had given in to His human nature and beaten the Roman soldiers who mocked Him and placed a crown of thorns upon His head? Would the plan of God still have happened? I don't know.

One thing I knew, Jesus was obedient to His father, and nothing—not a mockery, not a crown put on His head, not spit, and not a crucifixion—was enough to distract Him from accomplishing His mission. I thanked God for allowing me to focus on Him at work and not on any distractions around me to overcome evil plans.

When I got my visa, I realized God had a plan to move me to the United States of America. I also realized my story was like Joseph's story in the Bible. I remembered that Joseph's brothers hated him so much that they threw him into the pit. I was not thrown into a pit, but I was fired from my job, then went to play in a lottery, which resulted in my winning and obtaining a visa to go live in the United States of America.

In my case, I stayed faithful to God like Joseph. I did not become a prime minister like Joseph, but I did become a pillar to my family like Joseph. I was selected among more than ten million people who played the DV-2002 lottery in 2002. The total selection for the entire world was fifty thousand people, and I was among the seven hundred and seventy-five selected in Cameroon by God's grace.

I praised the Lord. Isaiah 25:1 (NIV) says, "Lord, you are my God; I will exalt you and praise your name, for in perfect faithfulness you have done wonderful things, things planned long ago."

I felt rejected like Joseph, and I was very desperate, not knowing what my future held. Yes, God may make us go through a painful situation to accomplish His plan in our lives.

There were situations where the Lord used evildoing done against me to transform to good, and there were situations where the Lord used my efforts, my accomplishments, and my commitment to turn it into good as well. He was the one who caused all things to work for good.

Genesis 50:20 (NASB) states, "As for you, you meant evil against me, but God meant it for good in order to bring about this present result, to preserve many people alive."

In the midst of this, the Lord was able to restore my joy by giving me back my job and everything I lost. He prepared my heart, like Joseph, to be able to love once against the very people that tried to hurt me.

CHAPTER 32

Unnecessary Worries

The Lord was working His plan behind the scenes through my persecution in the workplace. My plan was not always God's plan because when I finally got dismissed from my job, I almost lost control and my faith. The burden of losing my job overwhelmed me, and it was impossible for me to conceive the idea of being fired. My life's plan was going south. I thought everything was over for me.

I concluded that I would never be able to leave Cameroon. The reason I lost control was also that a lot of thoughts were going through my mind, but I did not have any answers for those thoughts.

One of my main concerns was the question of employment. Finding a job in Cameroon was like trying to get blood out of a stone. The employment problem was giant for me because my firing had consequences, such as stopping my plan and my dream to save and use the money to leave the country.

It would also limit my life perspective and hope. This concern really overwhelmed me at a point where I almost gave up, but the Lord did what He always does best. He brought me back to the scripture I had memorized about David and Goliath.

We all know the story. David defeated a giant not because he was stronger but because God in him was stronger than the giant, Goliath. It was understandable because I thought getting my first job was somehow by my own strength. It was not true because my strength in looking for a job wore out a long time ago after multiple attempts to find one. I prayed and fasted for my first job. I thought it would be impossible for me to go through another five years of job searching like I did for my first job.

Jesus said in Mark 9:23 (NKJV), "If you can believe, all things are possible to him who believes."

In Philippians 2:13 (AMP), the Lord said, "For it is, not your strength, but it is God who is effectively at work in you, both to will and to work is, strengthening, energizing, and creating in you the longing and the ability to fulfill your purpose for His good pleasure."

So, according to me, it was impossible to get another job, but according to the Lord, it was possible for me to get another job through Him. My internal battle was settled.

When I was worried about how to get another job to fulfill my dream and my plan, the Lord had another plan, and that was the reason He got me fired in the first place. Because after I got fired, I went straight to Douala and played the lottery, which was my passport for the US.

There was another issue: joining the Cameroonian military.

I already mentioned what happened and how I was scammed during the military recruitment back in Cameroon in 2000. My main concern was why life was not going my way after I failed to be recruited. My chance to join the military was now zero, given the fact that the age limit was twenty-two. I was way over the age limit, and it seemed like the end of the world to me. It was very difficult for me to wrap my mind around the concept of not being able to do what I loved.

Since my mind did not accept the fact that I could not join Cameroonian's military, especially because of my age, I started to think of myself as a loser. The enemy used this opportunity to show me all types of limitations in my life. I spent my time ruminating about things going bad in my life, and this brought me to stew in a situation I did not have any control over, which did not help me at all.

I realized that beating myself up for the past would not change anything, and once again, the Lord told me it is impossible with man but possible with Him.

I also went as far as to ask why the Lord let me be used and abused by the captain to such a degree and why I was blind during the scam process. I was able to answer my own question—my blindness was the result of wanting something so bad I could not see God's signs and listen to His voice.

I remembered when the Lord used His little voice in me to tell me it was a scam after I noticed the letter the captain gave me. The letter claimed to be from his friend, the head recruiter in my region, but was written by the captain to prove to me that the process was following his normal course. Still, after clear revelation, I could not take any stand or just quicken the process altogether because my blindness outweighed the voice of God and all the signs in front of me.

I had a lot of experience during my walk with the Lord where all the signs were pointing to my failure, but the desire of my heart outweighed any reasoning, and worse, the voice of God. I believed I needed to try to be a better listener to God's voice or my gut feeling next time around.

I also debated with myself if my intention to join the military had been wrong from the start. I knew the age limit was twenty-two, and I was twenty-seven, but it did not stop me. I thought that since anything was possible in Cameroon, the captain could manage to help me join the military, even though I didn't know how he would go about doing it. Since it did not work, I turned to God and started to wonder if my failure was a punishment for my complicity in committing fraud or something else.

The Lord never punished me for anything, but He would let me face the consequences of my sins.

Desperate people do desperate things, but I would later regret not being faithful to the Lord by not holding myself to His standard. It was wrong to try to double play on the age limit, and I tried to have another person do the dirty work for me. If I could do it again, I would do it differently. I asked the Lord to forgive me. I knew that He forgave me and that all my concerns about my activities during the military recruitment would not matter anymore.

The Lord later gave me the desire of my heart, which was to join the military, but this time it was God's choice. I crossed to a different continent and country where justice and equality were at the heart of the culture to realize my dream. The US would be a country where age and discrimination would not be a problem.

I wanted to leave Cameroon to go to a European country because I would easily adjust once there because of the language. But the United States of America was not on my list of countries to go to because I believed it was out of my league, and the language was part of my concern. The Lord decided otherwise. I dreamed, and I went for it, and the Lord saw my heart and blessed me. I resolved to be resilient and stayed in prayer because the Lord reminded me that worry would not change anything in my life.

Philippians 4:6 (NIV) states, "Do not be anxious about anything, but in every situation, by prayer and petition, with thanksgiving, present your requests to God."

He knew that the plan He had for me in the United States of America was to join the greatest military in the entire world. I worried about things that did not belong to me. I worried about things that I could not control. I worried about my future. I worried about Rachel not laughing enough. I made it my job to change her. I worried about; you name it (just add your name).

When the Lord said to me, "Do not worry or be anxious about anything," He was saying that worry was not part of His plan or His will for my life. If it was God's plan, then instead of worrying, I would be in peace and happier.

My plan was to save money to leave Cameroon or to join the military, and since it didn't work, I worried. It was a matter of trust, dependence, and belief. If it was possible to measure my worry, it could have gone from the earth to the sky and back ten times. The Lord had my back, and He was working a plan for a job, for the military, and for the US.

I believed the Lord felt very sorry for me when He saw me worrying because a greater and better plan, better than my plan, was coming my way.

I carried the worthless habit of worrying to the US, even when I saw the Lord's miracle. I worried about what I was going to do after the two years of military fireman work were completed. But the Lord had a job for me, which was religious program specialist. This would somewhat help me get out of my anxiety.

In addition, my first deployment in the Persian Gulf was another episode and almost brought me down to depression. I was very concerned about leaving my pregnant wife, who came from a French-speaking country and who couldn't express herself in English. It was also true for the second deployment as well, but in either case, the Lord had already made a plan for her to provide her with a wonderful lady, Mrs. Lynda.

Worry is part of who I am, but worrying about the things I did not have any control over was unnecessary. It was destructive to my relationship with Jesus and to my health.

I always remember that worry is the opposite of trust and belief, without which I could not please the Lord Jesus Christ.

Paul said in Hebrews 11:6 (NIV), "But without faith, it is impossible to [walk with God and] please Him, for whoever comes [near] to God must [necessarily] believe God exists and that he rewards those who [earnestly and diligently] seek Him."

All God wanted from me was to trust, believe, hope, depend, and obey by putting His word into action. I have faith in what He had promised He would do in my life.

Lastly, I learned through worry and tribulation because I was looking at the storm and not the One who calms the raging seas. I learned how to replace worries with prayers the hard way.

I tried to obey the Lord no matter what, follow, and take His Word very seriously because the Word of God is profound in the sense that it always accomplishes His purpose. Worries could have jeopardized my faith in the Lord, and the enemy's objective of weakening my faith in the Lord would be reached.

I could imagine Joseph worrying about his future and a lot of other things when he was thrown in prison. He didn't know what the future held for him or that the Lord was at work behind the scenes to bless him beyond measure. Just like Joseph, I worried. I worried about being fired, not knowing that it was God at work.

Instead of using my energy to worry about things I did not have any control over, which would not yield any fruits or, worse, may damage my health, I used that same energy to pray and enjoy the fruits.

Worry is for the Lord; put everything into His hand.

CHAPTER 33

Culture Shock

There were many wonderful things in the US, such as cleanliness, good roads, access to clean water, facilities to create a business, easy access to education, easy access to employment, etc. The only thing I found difficult was the social part of the culture.

It was easy in Cameroon to find people to interact with. Neighbors were accessible, and I did not need to make an appointment before I visited any of my neighbors because we had an open-door visitation policy.

Also, we had an open-market concept and a lot of social events, which helped me to interact with whomever I wanted. This, in turn, helped me a lot with my social needs, which also helped me to be emotionally stable.

In addition, we had at least five events at the church every week, such as prayer, evangelization, Bible study, etc. In the US, everything was different. Churches did not have a lot of events during the week. The food stores were different because I could not interact with anybody except the cashier, so most of the time, I just went in and grabbed whatever I wanted, and I paid for it and got out.

I even tried to join the Cameroonian community in Virginia, but they just met once a month. There was a lot of drama during those meetings, which was against my values. So after years of living in the US, it was still very difficult to adjust to the culture without socialization because I was looking for a living environment like Cameroon, and there was not one. I became depressed and sat in a corner.

At one point, I felt so lonely I went to see a doctor, who diagnosed me with adjustment disorder. Even though integrating into the workforce and making a living was easy, loneliness and being apart from my family still had an effect on me. There was medication for my diagnosis, but I preferred not to take any medications. I missed the social part of Cameroon's culture, and I knew an advanced culture would be different. I knew I would need to adapt to new patterns of behavior, but I did not think it would be a culture shock.

Other than loneliness, I did my best to integrate into the US culture. I barely knew my neighbors, and the only family I had were Rachel and our two beautiful daughters, and later our daughter Abira, who would come a little late in my life in 2016.

But I was amazed by the opportunity the country offered to its citizen, unlike Cameroon, where seventy-one percent of its citizens live in poverty, earn under five dollars and fifty cents a day, and many people over the age of twenty-five are still living with their parents because they have no means to live by themselves.

It is true that Cameroon is still a young country, but it has a long way to go for its development. As an immigrant, I was able to buy my first house and a car within two years of moving to the US. The Lord tremendously blessed this country, and I believe a lot of people do not realize how blessed they are to be here in the US. I was able to find a job in just a few weeks after receiving my work permit, which I did with little effort. But I noticed that some young folks—Black, White, you name it—did not want to work with all the opportunities offered to them, but instead, they wanted everything for free. As opposed to me, who decided to grab any opportunity.

Opportunities such as jobs, education, hands-on training, and business openings are there for anyone to grab. It was inconceivable for me to see young American-born citizens refusing to grab those opportunities. Instead of going running toward these opportunities, some decided to embrace laziness and reduce themselves to nothing.

There are millions of young men and women in Cameroon longing for the type of opportunities one finds in the US. There are no such opportunities in Cameroon, but young folks still manage to do something to survive instead of becoming a vagabond.

Most unemployed Cameroonians were holders of bachelor's and master's degrees, but it didn't stop them from selling water bottles on the street to survive. Generation after generation of well-educated citizens went to waste year after year. Unfortunately, Cameroon is not as blessed with good God-fearing leaders who are able to well manage the country's resources to create opportunities.

Most African countries are richly blessed with natural resources, but most are mired in poverty because of the poor and corrupt management of those resources. Lack of God-fearing government leaders and corruption continue to harm African countries and keep their people in poverty.

I came up with a plan for those in the US who do not want to work: Ship them to Cameroon for a period of six months, where life's misery is the laughingstock of man. I do believe they would come back with a new life perspective, and they would be straightened out. They would discover how blessed they are to have been born in the United States of America, and they would discover the opportunities they have here to live a better life.

They would discover that in Cameroon, there is no access to clean running water, constant loss of power, and a lack of jobs. Most people use their feet as a mode of transportation because there is no public transportation. Most houses have no modern bathroom. There are no social services to help the poor, no disability rights and law practices, and no justice. Tribalism is worse than racism. There are no modern hospitals, no ambulances to carry anyone to the hospital in case of an emergency, no freedom of expression, no liberty, and basically no life. They would run back to the United States like they had met their worst enemy or a monster in Cameroon.

I went on vacation in Cameroon in 2015 with my wife and our two daughters, Amarissa and Raya. My daughters do not want to go back there ever again because of the bad experience they had.

I strongly believe it would be the reaction of those people who did not want to work when they were sent to Cameroon. They would come back and have a different life perspective of this country. A country blessed beyond measure that offers the opportunity to all God's children and beyond. If you do not make it here in the United States of America, I do not think you would be able to make it elsewhere.

Throughout this book, my goal was not to compare Cameroon or Africa with any country but to use my experience living in Africa, especially in Cameroon and in the US, to show that a fair or unfair system could be a blessing or a stumbling block to its citizens and to show to some young folks who do not want to work to build a better future for themselves by working as God requires us to do.

In 2 Thessalonians 3:10 (NIV), the Lord says, "For even when we were with you, we would give you this command: If anyone is not willing to work, let him not eat."

I visited Europe, and there were no countries in the entire world that were welcoming like the United States of America.

I came here in 2002, and by 2004, I was established like any other United States citizen in the country. My integration was smooth, even with my language barrier, because it was easy for me to find a job even though it was not always what I had dreamt of. I purchased a car and a house. I was helped by the locals, by the state, friends, and by the federal government throughout my integration.

By comparison, this was not true for Europe. I have had a family member in France for more than forty years, and I visited him. He lived in a two-bedroom apartment, but he was impressed when he visited me in the United States of America because he saw that I owned a two-level, three-bedroom house. He told me he could not accomplish in forty years in France what I had accomplished in less than two years in the US.

I did not try to brag about myself, but I tried to make people understand that the opportunities here in the United States are overwhelming compared to other countries in the world.

So I ask myself this question: Why was it easy for me to make a life for myself, find a job, and buy a home when some people born in the US cannot? I was not the only one asking the question. Most foreigners I know ask the same question.

I concluded that everything came down to culture and heritage. I learned at an early age that education and hard work would determine the kind of man I would become in life. I did not necessarily learn from my parents alone, but I learned it from our culture as well. The Lord even made clear in the Bible that if you do not work, you do not get to eat. Joseph was an example of a hard-working man.

CHAPTER 34

Return to God's Love

In the United States of America, where milk and honey were God's blessing into my life, it was also a divine act of God to confuse the people who mocked me during the years of my miseries and said I would not be successful in life. Family members, friends, and neighbors had professed a lot of things about my life and my future, which turned out not to be true. They judged my future based on my previous conditions because they could not see my future. The Lord had proven them wrong because He was the one who knew my future and the plan He had for me. All these things professed about and against me got under my skin at one point in my life, and I started to believe the lies.

The Lord quickly changed my life perspective when I gave my life to Him, and I stopped being bothered by what people said and declared in my life. In addition, the Lord would bless me beyond measure by changing my life story.

At one point, I felt like those blessings became a curse. Since I had everything here in the United States of America, I started to lose my grip on what was important. I could not grow anymore in my faith, and worse, I started to backslide from my original commitment to my Lord because of my complacency.

I went from being a man of God to being a man without God because I was losing my grip on things that I once cherished and loved and loving the things of this world. I was always reminded by the Lord Jesus that I was taking the wrong path, and He was ready to welcome me back home at any time. Time after time, I had some type of spiritual awakening, and I would go to church like any other Christian, but I was still completely separated from the source of life, Jesus Christ, and it was not until I started to drop to a lower level of my moral standards that I decided that was it. I had gone astray, and now it was time to go back home by the grace of the Lord. I began to return to my daily Christian life routine.

Just like the prodigal son, I needed to come back to a stable environment, which was the body of Christ, where I could be spiritually fed, play my role in advancing the kingdom of Christ, serve the church through my natural and spiritual gifts and abilities, and keep my momentum for the love of God going.

First Corinthians 12:27 (NIV) states, "Now you are the body of Christ, and each one of you is a part of it."

I went to different churches during these hard times, but I did not become a member of any of them for the simple reason that they did not fit my church criteria. I strongly believed the devil had me where he wanted me to be: not going to church. My problem was that I looked for a church like my previous church in Cameroon instead of looking for a church where I could use my talents to serve. In the meantime, I was wasting the gifts the Lord had given me. I even thought of the idea of building a relationship with the Lord without going to church.

Since I could not find any church, even though there were thousands out there to choose from, I just kept procrastinating. It held me back from accomplishing the purpose the Lord had for my life, and the procrastination served the enemy instead. Glory be to God because the seed of the Word of God planted in me was greater than the love of things of this world, and nothing was going to separate me from God's love.

I renewed my love for Christ by starting to obey God's commandments again. I started my daily devotions once again, which included reading Scripture to strengthen my faith and relationship with God. Scripture should be like daily bread. I started listening to Him again and showing my gratitude for what He had done in my life. Even in my low moments, God was still with me. And I also started to stay close to the Lord throughout each day again and kept my heart and mind on Him.

Something was obvious even in my tribulations; He was always there trying to rescue me through His love, but I kept hardening my heart because I thought I was unworthy of His love. I had abused His love before, and I might do it again, but I forget that the Lord is bigger. He had me in mind all this time as I was wandering.

Something started tugging at my soul to find a safe faith space in which I could heal, grow, and stir up the spiritual gifts inside of me. After more than three years, I decided to become a member of a local Norfolk church in my neighborhood. But it was a big church, unfortunately, and it was impossible to see the pastor except on Sunday on the podium, and even the process of being a member was complicated, given my work schedule. But there was another branch of the Norfolk church in Chesapeake, Virginia, where I finally settled.

The Chesapeake church was run by a different pastor, and he was accessible. The congregation was small, and we even had a small prayer group. Even though it was nothing like my church back home, I stayed for the good of my soul because the church focused on the

teaching of Jesus' love, fellowship, holiness, and forgiveness. I wanted to make a difference in people's lives
as much I could by using the gifts the Lord has blessed
me with.

I served the Lord in church for years in any capacity
I could, and my revival became real, and I saw myself
connecting back with the Lord Jesus once again. I went
from a lifeless life journey to a purposeful life. Once you
have tested the love of God and His goodness in your
life, it is very difficult to live a life apart from Him.
My life away from the Lord was like walking through a
thornbush where I was getting hit with various shrubs
or with spines, and I thought it would get better as soon
I got out of the thornbush. Except I could not get out
the thornbush by my own strength, but I thanked the
Lord for coming to my rescue.

I left the Calvary Chesapeake Church around September 2013 to move to Richmond, where Rachel had
gotten a new job as a nurse at McGuire Medical Center.
I understood the importance of being part of a church
family, and I first joined the Grace Bible Church and
then Passion Community Church (PCC), where I stayed.

When I look back at the apostle era in the Bible, there
were not many churches to choose from, and people
were lucky to have a church in their neighborhood. They
endured a lot of persecution to even have a church. In
my case, the enemy had successfully used the fact that I

was looking for a church like my previous home church to restrain me from settling in a good Bible-preaching church.

I made the mistake of not settling a little early in a church. I felt complacent and comfortable in my sin because it was easy, tempting, pleasurable, and felt good until I could not bear it anymore. I made the mistake of putting the desires of flesh upon my spirituality over the desire of God for me. As a matter of fact, my spiritual needs should have taken precedence over anything else in my life.

In Richmond, I joined a local church, but everything was done according to their tradition, and there was no room for free expression and no freedom to serve. I resolved to find another church as soon as possible that I could be part of. I loved serving. So by the grace of God, my family and I were driving on a Sunday morning searching for a new church around the neighborhood, and we were fortunate to see PCC's sign on the street. As was our practice, we went to visit the church the next Sunday.

My family and I were amazed by the reception first and later by the message given by the senior pastor. This was the end of our home church search. It was very difficult, especially for me, to love a church because I was still emotionally and spiritually attached to my Cameroon church, but the similarity in loving, preaching, and small group Bible study practice sealed my faith in PCC.

My first and lasting impression of PCC was the welcome team at the entrance of the church. They extended their hands and looked me in the eye. They smiled, and it broke down my apprehensiveness. It showed me that I mattered and that I was accepted, and it established in me a mood that enabled me to worship. Before I even left the church, I was already thinking about the next Sunday, in which I believed the next message would help change my life and help me grow in the Lord.

The pastor was gifted in sharing the message in a way in which I could identify myself in the message. I had my needs, and I needed to feel connected to the message. I needed that connection to be genuine, authentic, and realistic in the struggles I faced daily.

My faith and love for PCC were completely sealed with a small group. No matter the size of the church, I need to be in a small community of believers where I can grow more, be accountable, socialize, be supported, contribute, learn, and know I can be helped when things are going rough in my life.

The small group was very valued in PCC, and it was a top priority for me when I was looking for a local church where I could serve. Today, I am part of the welcome team to extend a smile to create a welcoming and friendly environment where members and newcomers can experience Christ. I am very happy to be a member of PCC because my family and I can praise and worship and understand life's most important priority.

PCC offers us the power to center on what really matters and inspire us for the week ahead. It helps us connect with the body of the believer, be and stay in the body of Christ, and be part of something bigger than ourselves. It helps us with our spiritual, emotional, and physical needs.

PCC is also a family center church where we take care of each other, where we pray together, laugh and cry together. It is a church that helps families, men, and women build a strong foundation in Christ.

CHAPTER 35

Giving Back

I asked some questions to a friend at my church, PCC, about the American culture of hospitality. They told me there were no set of rules on hospitality in the US, and every situation was different and required different accommodation.

I asked this question because I believed two to twelve weeks of hospitality was not enough, especially for someone coming from a foreign country to the US to live and build a life. This didn't mean I was ungrateful for the length of time Paul and my cousin kept me in their homes, but I was being realistic. Two to twelve weeks was not enough for a foreigner to fully integrate into the American culture, which requires knowing how to drive, speak English for those who were not bilingual, and get a job.

I believed the Lord allowed me to go through the experience to bless someone else seeking to come and live in the US. My plan was to help immigrants who reached out to me for help, not the whole world.

As soon as Rachel moved to the US, I moved off the ship, and we rented an apartment for a year, and later, we bought our first house with three bedrooms and one and a half bathrooms in Norfolk. We were ready to help as soon we got settled. We helped a lot of people for years. The average time of hospitality we gave to immigrants to stay with us was eight months or more, and we helped them to fully integrate into the American culture. The process was time-consuming.

Helping immigrants consisted of providing them with an affidavit of support for visa application, and once they obtained a visa and moved to the US, we provided them with a place to stay. We helped them fill out the application for a social security number; I taught them how to drive, and we helped them find a job as soon as they received their social security and green cards. I had to drive them back and forth from school or their job until they were able to drive themselves.

In Cameroon, we barely had any bills, but it was a very different situation here in the US because bills almost killed me, and the bills for our house, such as utilities, electricity, and water, would change every time we had someone added to our family. It was a sacrifice for my family and me, but we were happy to do it in the name of God. We welcomed at least four Cameroonian immigrants into our house, and we were not related to most of them. We even helped people that were not Cameroonians.

At one point, there was a family of seven, along with the eight people already in our home, making a total of fifteen people in a three-bedroom house. People slept on the couch, in the office, or any place they could find to lie down. The living situation was not always easy, but because all of them were Christians, it helped us stay and pray together and love each other. The joy of helping outweighed everything else, even the bills.

Matthew 10:42 (CSB) says, "Whoever gives even a cup of cold water to one of these little ones because he is a disciple, truly I tell you, he will never lose his reward."

Cameroon was a society in which family included children, parents, grandparents, and cousins living together. Their relationships were very strong, and their obligations to each other ran profoundly. Family members gave respect to the elderly, and retirement homes were not part of the living concept because we took care of each other, so it was natural for me to help those folks without any complaisance.

I share these testimonies not to boast about the good I did for people in need but to prove that everything in life happens for a reason. Since I was subjected to a treatment I believed was not right, or the help did not fit His purpose to integrate in the US, I concluded that it was my responsibility to change the course by making things right for other people by helping them.

Matthew 7:12 (NIV) states, "So in everything, do to others what you would have them do to you, for this sums up the Law and the Prophets."

I like to believe that it is in my relationship with others that one sees my Christlike features, especially the traits of kindness, love, and hospitality like Joseph.

Just as God richly blessed Joseph, He still has many promises coming my way. If you have accepted Jesus as your Savior and learned to lean on Him, the miracle worker, the same will be true for you.

CPSIA information can be obtained
at www.ICGtesting.com
Printed in the USA
BVHW041332051221
623253BV00004B/10